GOD AND US

a life-changing adventure

To my wife Judy,
and our children Luke and Anna-Marie,
who have been my cherished partners in
my exploration of God

GOD AND US

a life-changing adventure

Keith Warrington

© Keith Warrington 2004
First published 2004
ISBN 1 85999 698 1

Scripture Union, 207-209 Queensway,
Bletchley, Milton Keynes, MK2 2EB, England
Email: info@scriptureunion.org.uk
Website: www.scriptureunion.org.uk

Scripture Union Australia
Locked Bag 2, Central Coast Business Centre, NSW 2252
Website: www.su.org.au

Scripture Union USA
P.O. Box 987, Valley Forge, PA 19482
Website: www.scriptureunion.org

All Scripture quotations, unless otherwise indicated, are taken from the Holy
Bible, New International Version, © 1973, 1978, 1984 by International Bible
Society. Anglicisation © 1979, 1984, 1989. Used by permission of Hodder and
Stoughton Limited.

British Library Cataloguing in Publication Data.
A catalogue record of this book is available from the British Library.

Cover design by David Lund
Printed and bound by Creative Print and Design (Wales), Ebbw Vale

✏ Scripture Union is an international Christian charity working with
churches in more than 130 countries, providing resources to bring the
good news about Jesus Christ to children, young people and families and to
encourage them to develop spiritually through the Bible and prayer.
    As well as our network of volunteers, staff and associates who run holidays,
church-based events and school Christian groups, we produce a wide range of
publications and support those who use our resources through training programmes.

Contents

Introduction

A little boy once asked God how long a million years was to him. God replied, 'A million years to me is just like a single second to you.'

The little boy asked God what a million pounds was to him. God replied, 'A million pounds to me is just like a single penny to you.'

Then the little boy asked, 'God, can I have one of your pennies?'

God smiled and said, 'Certainly. Just wait a second.'

If there's one thing you can say about God, it's this: he's different. The amazing thing is that he invites us to explore him.

This book came about as a result of listening to my wife, Judy. She said, 'We don't hear enough sermons about God.' Her assessment was accurate. We hear sermons about how to be a better Christian; how to pray better; how to share the gospel more effectively; how to read the Bible enjoyably; how to be a better father, mother, son, daughter, husband, wife, pastor, elder. The list is endless. But sermons on God are comparatively rare. Is this because people have so many problems that need to be addressed in sermons? Or are we reflecting our age, which tends to be self-indulgent and focused on us, our concerns and our lives?

These issues have pushed aside the person of God so that he is largely undiscovered. The one who has established eternity for relationship with him is largely unknown and unexplored by many Christians. Yet he is the answer to many of our problems, and an investigation of his being may provide more answers for our contemporary dilemmas than we imagine.

But to attempt to explore the greatness of God is daunting. It would be impossible to scrutinise the wonders of the sea, to explore the unsearchable reaches of the universe, to probe every moment in the history of the world or analyse every intimate detail of creation. To attempt to explore God satisfactorily, let alone to complete the journey, is an impossibility that will defy even the endless aeons of eternity. But it is a voyage of delightful discovery and a privileged mission that has been granted to us, especially because the focus of our consideration takes us by the hand and opens himself to our gaze, allowing us an insight into the unimaginable.

Therefore, in the steps of others who have travelled as reverent adventurers into the greatness of God, I now tread. I hope to take you with me as we explore something of the mystery of the one who inhabits eternity because time is too small for him. This book will be an accessible, biblically based exploration of God with a personal and contemporary application. I hope to provide a stimulus to the intellect as well as to the emotions, with the aim of enabling you increasingly to realise the amazing nature of your God. Each chapter, which may be read in less than 15 minutes, includes some Bible references to ensure faithfulness to Scripture, and concludes with poetry that attempts to encapsulate the chapter's theme, followed by discussion questions to tease out some of the implications of the topic. The 12 main chapters are presented in couplets so that readers can explore, in parallel, issues that are associated with each other.

1 He's creative

Have you ever wondered:

- how God created something out of nothing?
- why God created humanity?
- how we can measure God's intelligence?
- how anyone can create a planet called Earth that weighs 66,000,000,000,000,000,000,000,000 tons?

God's creativity expresses his freedom

The Bible does not explore how God created, but it is emphatic in declaring that he did create and that he chose to do so freely. No one encouraged God to create. No one suggested the idea to him. It was not something that he had to do. Before God created anything and anyone, he existed in perfect, self-sufficient contentment. God needs nothing outside of himself. With this in mind, his creation of the world is a remarkable act of golden grace.

God's creativity reflects beauty

On a beautiful day when the world was waiting and the angels were watching, God created human life that reflected him. Adam and Eve were sparkling new. As with everything he had already created, his human creation was without comparison; it was good, exquisite and beautiful. Beauty exists because of God, whether it's the beauty of a butterfly, the awesome sight of a mountain range, a breathtaking sunset or a soft snowflake. Each is excellent in its own way, to be admired because it is exceptional.

God's creativity reflects meticulous precision

The chances of the Earth meeting the exact criteria needed
for life to occur on it are astronomically small. God creates
perfectly because he is wise (Ps 104:24; Prov 3:19). The Old
Testament pictures of creation point to a Creator who may be
depended on to create a perfectly designed and functionally
reliable creation. The terms the Old Testament uses reflect a
master craftsman or peerless designer who creates something
carefully planned and perfectly executed (Job 38:4–6). Not only
do his creative abilities not tire him; they are also way beyond
our understanding (Isa 40:28; Rom 11:33–36).

There is precision about the creation of the Earth. The angle
of its tilt (23.5° from the perpendicular) as it turns gives us the
different seasons. If the tilt were less, much of the Earth would
be uninhabitable. If the tilt were greater, extreme temperatures
would make life intolerable. The speed of the Earth's rotation
around the Sun (365 days, 5 hours, 48 minutes and 45.51 sec-
onds, exactly) ensures that wind speeds on Earth are beneficial,
unlike the climate of Jupiter, which rotates twice as quickly as
the Earth, causing wind speeds of up to 1,000 miles an hour. A
faster rotation would result in the Earth moving away from the
Sun; a slower rotation would result in the opposite.

The balance between nitrogen, oxygen, argon and carbon
dioxide in the air is just right for human life to be maintained.
Although carbon dioxide comprises only 0.03 per cent of the
atmosphere, it is crucial to life on Earth, for it is required by
plants, trapping the Sun's radiation and enabling them to grow.
If there were less carbon dioxide, plant life would decrease,
resulting in less food for animals, and the food cycle would
spiral downwards. An increase in carbon dioxide would cause a
significant increase in temperature. The careful balance in the
atmosphere acts as a giant protective umbrella. Without it, the
Earth would be subject to a constant bombardment of meteors
that would destroy life, but instead they burn up in the atmosphere.

The Earth's distance from the Sun is crucial to our existence. A few million miles closer and the glaciers would melt, causing the sea level to rise and cities and islands to be flooded. The increased sea cover would result in greater evaporation, and the increased release of water vapour and carbon dioxide would further raise the temperature of the world. If the Sun were further away, the opposite would occur, and the world would freeze to death. The ozone layer is the right thickness to keep out harmful ultraviolet rays from the Sun while letting in sufficient heat for us to live.

For many in the developed world, water is taken for granted. However, it is very rare in the Universe. In fact, it is known to exist only on Earth. The Earth has it in significant quantities, estimated at 340 million cubic miles, covering 71 per cent of the Earth's surface. Its physical and chemical properties provide an ideal environment as a primary component of life. One of its main functions is as a worldwide air conditioner, keeping the temperature of the land at a bearable level, the currents cooling the equatorial land and waters and warming the polar regions. It also acts as an effective recycling organism. Most of the Earth's carbon dioxide is dissolved in it, including the vast amounts created by the burning of fossil fuels, which would otherwise be released into the atmosphere, with cataclysmic consequences.

Another remarkable property of water is evident when it cools. As with most other materials, as it cools it contracts. But when the temperature sinks to 4°C it starts to expand – in contrast to most other materials – until it freezes. Ice then floats to the surface. If water continued to contract instead of expanding, it would become heavier, and ice would form on the *bottom* of the oceans, in the process killing many fish and lowering the temperature of the water until the sea froze from the bottom up.

The size and density of the Earth, the thickness of its crust, the fact that the Earth exists because of the Sun, its closeness to the Sun, the size and brightness of the Sun – these and many other features indicate that the creation is complex and precisely ordered. God is meticulous in all he does, exact in all he is.

He creates because he is God, because he is unselfish and
wants to bless what he creates with his presence. He creates so
that his creation can receive his smile. Those whom he forms
feel his pleasure. Whatever he causes to come into being is
crafted out of his desire to care for his craftsmanship. His creativity is channelled into being because of love alone.

The personal involvement of God in his creation is reflected
in the way he creates. In picture language, the writers describe
him using his fingers (Ps 8:3), shaping the mountains and creating the wind (Amos 4:13). His intimacy with his creation is demonstrated by the fact that it reflects him (Ps 8:1; 19:1) and praises
him (Ps 104:31,32). God does not create in order to receive praise
as if he needed it. Rather, what he creates is described as spon-
taneously and naturally expressing its pride at being created in
such a perfect way by such a perfect Creator. The sixteenth-cen-
tury Reformer John Calvin described creation as the theatre of
God's glory. When we examine God's creation we recognise
what a remarkable God he is. However, although his creation
remains perfect when in relationship to the Creator, when the
relationship is marred the creation is impaired. Sin has dam-
aged God's creation, which longs to be renewed (Rom 8:21).

God does not absent himself from his creation

Psalm 104 tells us the trees are cared for by God (v 16) and young
lions and fish depend on him (vs 21,25–27). When the writer to
the Hebrews speaks of God's involvement with his creation, he
states that through his Son he sustains it (1:3). He is not a giant
Atlas who holds the world on his shoulders. Rather, his role
as Sustainer describes not his strength but his authority. God
controls the destiny of the world, determining its end from its
beginning. He is not an absentee landlord but a governing God.
Paul says God holds all things together continuously (Col 1:17).
Jesus develops a similar theme, reminding his hearers that God
cares for the inconsequential sparrow so they have no need to

worry (Luke 12:6). Similarly, Peter reminds his readers, who are suffering persecution, that the Creator is faithful to those whom he has created (1 Pet 4:19).

God's creativity inspires worship

On 20 July 1969, Apollo 11 touched down on the Moon. For the first time, people could observe the Earth from another celestial body. The pictures beamed back were remarkable. Earth offers some remarkable sights, but the Universe is breathtaking. Although incompletely surveyed (there are probably over a hundred billion galaxies in the Universe), what has been discovered provides an overwhelming backdrop to the Earth, filling believers with humility and awe. The Sun is just one example of God's creation. Its energy is so enormous that the Earth harnesses only one billionth of its daily output. The Bible presents the unimaginable nature of God's creation in picture language. It describes him stretching out the heavens like a tent (Ps 104:2), scattering frost (Ps 147:16), holding the winds in his fist (Prov 30:4) and wrapping the oceans in his cloak (Prov 30:4).

God's creativity reflects him, and his creation carries an imprint of him. The more we consider creation, the more we are drawn to its Creator. Creation is one of his ways of getting our attention and transforming us into a congregation of watching worshippers. The more we examine the world and the Universe, the more we are moved to consider the magnitude and character of its Creator. God creates as a manifestation of his being. It is a defining element of his person. There is a mystery about the Universe. For instance, why do Venus and Uranus rotate in the opposite direction to the other planets in our solar system? Like his Universe, God's character has deep caverns of mystery.

Imagine the first day of creation. The angels are waiting and watching; they know something amazing is going to take place. Then God starts, and, in an explosion of colour and sounds, the Universe floods over the darkness. It's splendid. It's awesome.

It's God. Sparkling stars send pulses of light towards him; massive meteors move towards him and wait for his word of command; dazzling sunlight from a myriad stunning suns squeezes the darkness out of the scene. And the angels are astounded as he starts to create. In the words of the psalmist,

In his hand are the depths of the earth,
and the mountain peaks belong to him.
The sea is his, for he made it,
and his hands formed the dry land.
Come, let us bow down in worship;
let us kneel before the LORD *our maker.*
(Ps 95:4–6)

God is still creating

The days of creation have not finished. The Creator is still creating. He's moving, stirring, tireless and enthusiastic in all he does. Lamentations 3:23 records that '[his compassions] are new every morning.' Isaiah states, 'See, I am doing a new thing!' (43:19), and 'From now on I will tell you of new things' (48:6). The psalmist (40:3) proclaims, 'He has put a new song in my mouth.' He is the God of the now as well as of the past; the God of the new as well as of the old. He is the active God, who intimately involves himself in our lives. He does not sit idly by and watch the world from a distance. Rather, he dynamically moves within our lives.

God's creativity is reflected in us

Although we are different from God, we share his characteristic of creativity. Just as God enjoys creating, so he has blessed us with the capacity to be creative. Genesis records that when God created the various elements of the world, he pronounced each of them good. A similar prospect, that of enjoying our creativity, awaits each believer created in his likeness.

Although God does not change, he creates change, developing new life, fresh experiences, unique lessons, innovative opportunities, progressive adventures, imaginative prospects and life destinies for us; creating what we shall be out of what we were. Our responsibility as believers is to gaze into the future with the recognition that a creative God is planning it. With the Spirit as our guide, and after identifying our gifts, strengths and passions, the next step should be to determine how to creatively develop frameworks for change within our lifestyles. Some of us may wish to write songs, learn to play an instrument, master an art form, engage in political life, develop social programmes, write a book or an article or research a subject. The list is potentially endless – projects to see through, trips to make, people to see, new habits to form. It can be broad-based and result in a two-year plan for change; it can be more narrowly focused on developing a greater vibrancy in our relationship with God; it can be relational or functional; it can be intimately personal or public.

The common denominator in each of these options is that they represent opportunities for change and a framework in which change can be achieved. Are we living in the present, realising that there is a future to be grasped, or living in the present as if the future didn't exist? AW Tozer wrote, 'Refuse to be average.' Only God knows the kind of person who is waiting to be developed within each believer, but, with his capacity to be creative, he encourages us to dream, and whispers, 'Be creative like your Creator.' Because of his creative artistry and wisdom, we should look for surprises with God.

Anyone can tell how many seeds are in an apple; only God can tell how many apples are in a seed. Take a leaf out of God's book and be creative, like your Creator.

He flung the stars out into space
and every one went to its place
and stayed.

He dropped the oceans in the sea.
The waters flowed obediently.
He tossed the sun and moon up high;
They shone for him in the darkened sky.

In his power and awesome might
he ordered the day to turn to night.
He commanded everything to be right,
for he, the Creator, ruled.

He reigned supreme, in splendour, awe.
His glory no one could endure.
And when the King whispered a word,
*   a myriad angels in glittering robes*
*   pounced to obey his every word,*
*   their King, their Lord.*

But he cradles us in his arms.
He joins us in our storms and gently calms our fears.
He steps into our shoes, just where we are.
He shepherds us with tender care,
*   with fingers, hands,*
*   love beyond compare.*

He flung the stars out into space,
but he welcomes us with a warm embrace.
He shows us a glimpse of his eternal grace,
to us – members of a fallen race.
The King has a smile upon his face,
for the Creator has made us his own.

Questions for discussion

1. Why did God create the world? (Col 1:16; Rev 4:11)
2. What does creation reveal about God? (Ps 19:1; Isa 45:18)

3. What does creation reveal about the significance of humanity? (Gen 5:1,2; Heb 2:6,7)

4. How does creation encourage our readiness to trust in God? (Deut 32:6; Isa 40:26; 43:7)

5. What lessons for our lifestyle can we learn from the way that God created? (Gen 1:21)

Questions to think about

1. Can we be certain that God created the world?

2. What are the most significant aspects of God's creation?

3. What difference should the fact that God created the Earth make to our lifestyles?

4. What targets can we set ourselves as we reflect our Creator and honour the creative capacity he has given us?

2 He gives himself to us

Have you ever wondered:

- what life would be like if we were not Christians?
- what the word 'grace' means?
- whether God has planned abilities for us in this life?
- what abilities God has given us?

There's something satisfying about completing a project, whatever it might be. You invest time and effort, perhaps at some personal cost, and when the task is completed, like a cat who's found a lifetime's supply of cream, you purr with contentment. You've been released to enjoy life again and to relax for a while. It's time to reward yourself. If you had a day free after a busy week of creativity, what would you choose to do?

After God had packed into a week what we could not do in an eternity of weeks, he had a day free. What would you do with that day if you were God? Have a break, a rest or a holiday? Would you spoil yourself, go shopping, have a day in the country or socialise? Or would you take on an even bigger project? That's what God did. After God created the world, he created people.

But this was not as easy as it seems. Creating people meant more potential problems than creating the Universe ever did, because people were created with the ability to say 'No' to God. God wanted to create people who could enjoy a relationship with him. But he did not want to force that relationship on them; he did not want robots, people programmed to love him. He wanted them to love him freely. That meant that they had to be free to leave his love as an unwanted gift, to say 'No, thank you,' to God.

And God gave people that choice. Why? It's because he wanted our relationship with him to be based on love, freely offered and freely received. To do that best, he allowed us to say 'No'.

But in order to start that relationship with us, all he expects us to say is 'Yes'. When we recognise our need of God's forgiveness, which Jesus achieved when he died on the cross, God says, 'Welcome.' He accepts us unconditionally. We give him nothing but our sins and ourselves; he gives us his forgiveness and himself. It's an unequal, unfair transaction, but he enters into it willingly. That's why the word 'grace' crops up so often in the Christian life. Everything that happens to us is proof of his grace. As CS Lewis wrote, 'God, who needs nothing, loves into existence wholly superfluous creatures in order that He may love and perfect them.'

Before

His gracious activity towards us pre-dates us by centuries – before we were born, before our parents were born, before anyone was born. Before people ever think about God, God has already thought about them. Before they start to feel their way towards him, he has stretched his hands down to them. Before they bow the knee, he bends his ear; before they express hope, he has left heaven; before they dare to say sorry, he has died to save them. Before anyone proceeds towards a relationship with God, God starts the process (1 Tim 1:9). He leads us to himself – we who cannot search for him, we who cannot even accidentally bump into him. God is the God of the previous, who finishes before we start, who says 'Hello' to us when we're hiding from him.

Not only that, but he chooses to be our friend at the cost of his Son. If God were to accept me into his family by a statement of his will, that would be more than I deserve. But to enable it to happen through the humiliation of becoming a created being, the scandal of being treated as a nobody, the outrage of a painful cross, the shame of bearing the punishment for my sins, the degrading of God, is more than I can understand. At unimaginable cost to himself, he freely gives us what we need (Eph 1:6). At this point, we just begin to open the door of the vast treasure stores of grace, God's gifts to us.

Paul is clear that Jesus, the Spirit and the Father demonstrate grace to Christians. We cannot understand the concept of the Trinity. But we are told that all the members of the Godhead are united in everything they do, especially when it relates to the support of the Christian. Jesus redeems and forgives us (Eph 1:7), the Spirit enables us to be a home for God (2:22) and the Father gives us eternal life (2:4). In 2 Corinthians 13:14 Paul writes his only benediction, in which each of the members of the God-head is mentioned: 'The grace of the Lord Jesus Christ and the love of God and the fellowship of the Holy Spirit be with you all.' Although God is a mystery, he wants us to recognise his commitment to us, and here Paul identifies aspects of this care. He is saying not that the individual attributes are restricted to particular members of the Godhead, but that all of them are intrinsically intertwined and all are dedicated to supporting us sensitively in every moment of our lives.

During

When a baby is born it enjoys the dedicated attention of a number of people, including hospital staff, parents, siblings, grandparents, friends – even the family dog, for a while. Through it all, the child is blissfully unaware that he or she has become the centre of a new world. This is natural when a baby is ushered into life with lavish love. Writing to the young Christians in Ephesus, Paul describes some of the gifts that God has lavished on them at the start of their Christian lives (1:8). He provides wisdom (1:17–19) and empowers them (3:16), while also giving gifts to them (4:7,8).

In a world of easy promises and empty pledges, it's natural to be sceptical regarding guarantees that seem too good to be true.

God's grace is one of those guarantees that seems too good to be true. Paul tells the Corinthians about one of these guarantees that God has given him: 'My grace is sufficient for you' (2 Cor 12:9).

When our children were much younger, we went for walks in the country. On one of these treks we crossed a stream that was too wide for their little legs. Although they had boundless energy, they lacked ability; they saw the other side, but focused on the gap. The crossing was easy for me, however, and because I carried them it was easy for them too. Similarly, God provides strength for our struggles, wisdom for our wilderness, love for our loneliness, friendship for our fear, forgiveness for our failure, hope for our heartache, joy for our journey and grace to reach the goal.

Paul makes a strange statement in Romans 8:26: 'the Spirit …intercedes for us'. That the Spirit prays for us is encouraging, because it's good to be aware that the Spirit is on our side. But the Spirit is God. So is God praying to himself? The Spirit can't be reminding God about my situation, because the Spirit is God. He can't be asking God for extra resources because, as God, he has them all already.

Paul is painting a picture with words to explore the fact that the Spirit in us works in partnership with the Father to support us in all our situations, not just when life is at its lowest but throughout all our days; when nightmares control our next steps; through the storms when all we can taste is our tears; in the hurricane when we hunt for a haven; and also when we can see a golden horizon, when dreams come true and life is too wonderful for words. God is there not just when we need him but also when we don't seem to. The Spirit is speaking out loud for our benefit so that we can hear his heartbeat for us.

The word used by Paul to describe the way the Spirit helps us is rare and includes the idea of support or partnership. He doesn't just help us from above, but comes alongside us and is with us; he steps into our shoes; not just once but continually and continuously. This is not support from a distance, not help from another world, but closer than a whisper. This word for 'help' is used once elsewhere in the New Testament, in Luke 10:40, where Martha asks for Mary to help her. She wants Mary to hold her hand in the helping process. God is so close that he can take our hand and charge us with his energy.

Within us

God doesn't just stand with us; he wants to work through us. Peter wrote to a group of Christians who knew what it was to feel unappreciated and impoverished. They had suffered for their faith and discovered that the world they lived in was an inhospitable place. They were alienated by its inhabitants; they belonged to another country, called heaven. Until they reached it, Peter told them, they must use the gifts they had received from God (1 Pet 4:10). The Greek word for 'gift' (*charisma*) comes from the same root as the word for 'grace' (*charis*). God's grace is reflected in us and activated in us in practical ways for the benefit of others.

When I was a young Christian and heard that God had given gifts to Christians, I pored over those listed by Paul (Rom 12:6–8; 1 Cor 12:8–10,28–30; Eph 4:11). But I couldn't identify any of them in me. I had never prophesied, spoken in tongues, given an interpretation or achieved any miracles or healings. I wasn't an apostle, pastor, teacher, evangelist or prophet. I had never ruled or shown much wisdom, never exhibited much knowledge. I faltered in my faith and didn't like giving too much. The conclusion was straightforward. When God looked in his barrel of gifts, he couldn't find one for me. Maybe he chose not to give me one. Who could blame him? If I were God I wouldn't have given one to me either! I didn't deserve one. I was just a young Christian, happy to be saved and knowing that I was going to heaven.

But then I discovered 1 Corinthians 12:4–7,11. I discovered that it wasn't because people were spiritual that God had given them his gifts, and that my task wasn't to ask for a gift from God but to discover what he had already given me and to use it. Paul's lists are not meant to be exhaustive; he is simply giving examples of God's activity in his people. I learnt that these gifts are varied. We are not to grab hold of them and tightly grasp them to ourselves. They are gifts from God to enable us to reflect something of his grace to others. Becoming a child of God involves becoming like a prism through which the greatness of God's generosity and the intimacy of his compassionate care are radiated to others who need to receive them. Exploring God's gifts to us helps us appreciate the meaning of grace, because not only do we not deserve them but we could not even receive them if God had not made it possible.

After

Next time you look at a mountain, tell yourself that when the mountain has been worn away by the winds of time you'll still be alive; when the sun has cooled into a block of ice you'll still be sparkling bright; when the rivers have all run dry you'll still be bubbling with life because God has planned eternity with you in mind. In giving himself to us he has changed us from what we were and is committed to transforming us into what he wants us to be – like him, so that we shall live our future in the fullness of his life. Our future is based on the fact that God is for us, unconditionally. That's grace. There's no satisfactory reason, no understandable explanation; it's a marvellous mystery and an inexhaustible journey of discovery.

Grace sums up God, who gives himself to us

The Father, Son and Spirit are committed to all aspects of our salvation. A wealthy English family were horrified one afternoon to hear that their young son Winston had nearly drowned in the swimming-pool. He was saved by the gardener. Years later, after Winston had become Prime Minister of England, he was stricken with pneumonia. The King called for the best doctor in England to ensure he recovered. The doctor was Alexander Fleming, the developer of penicillin and the son of the gardener who had saved him from drowning. Churchill had been saved by the father and the son.

God's commitment to us, however, is threefold, for not only has the Father saved us through the sacrifice of the Son but the Spirit guarantees to accompany us on our journey. One of the most famous paintings in the world is Leonardo da Vinci's *Mona Lisa*. One of its remarkable aspects is that her eyes seem to follow you wherever you stand in the room. God sees us not just from afar; he follows us with his eyes, hears our heartbeat, knows our name and stays with us when we stop.

One of the exercises I sometimes undertake with my students is to work through part of a Bible verse word by word. It's a form of meditation and allows them to savour the meaning of the words. God's promise to Paul, 'My grace is sufficient for you' (2 Cor 12:9) is a good example to practise on. Repeat the phrase aloud slowly, emphasising only one word every time you do, until you have spoken it six times (once for each word) and begun to explore some of its treasures. It will be our eternal destiny to explore his grace, so begin to enjoy it now.

When the world was dark and light was gone,
when creation groaned and the people mourned,
when evil creatures grinned and planned,
God stepped down and became a man.

When icy winds of fear and doubt
clutched at joy and threw it out
this world was lost and hope was gone.
But then, a child was born;
a child who sucked his thumb and smiled,
a boy who learned to sing and sigh,
a king who learned to fear and cry,
a baby who was born to die.

To show us God, to show us love,
his child stepped down from heaven above,
to say, 'I care, you're special to me.'
He left his throne where he reigned supreme
and came to earth so that we could see
his heart of grace for you, for me.

Questions for discussion

1. How has God shown his grace to you? (Rom 6:14; Eph 2:4–9; Titus 3:7; Heb 2:9)
2. How can you be certain that God has demonstrated his grace to you? (John 1:16; Rom 5:8; 2 Cor 8:9; Heb 4:16)
3. What are some New Testament evidences of God's grace in us? (Acts 14:3; 20:32; Rom 12:6; 2 Cor 9:8)
4. 1 Peter 5:10 describes God as 'the God of all grace'. What does this mean to you?
5. How can God's grace be reflected in us? (Col 4:6; 1 Pet 4:10)

Questions to think about

1. How can you ensure that you don't take the grace of God for granted?
2. Define the word 'grace'.
3. Identify an example of grace in the life of a Bible character.
4. How can you show grace to others today?

3 He lives in eternity

Have you ever wondered:

- what it means to say that God is eternal?
- whether eternity is more than endless time?
- how time and eternity relate to each other?
- whether eternal life gets better year after year?

Marshall Shelley is a husband and a father of five children, four girls and one boy, of whom three are living on this earth and two in heaven. Mandy was two weeks short of her second birthday when she entered eternity. Three months earlier, Toby had been born. He had departed from this life into eternity two minutes after he was born. Marshall Shelley and his wife struggled with the questions: Why would God create a child to live for two years, for two minutes? Why had God created a life that would last for only two minutes? They came to the conclusion that God had not created their daughter to live for two years. Neither had God created their son to live for two minutes. God had created them for eternity.

What a remarkable truth! God has created us not for two years, ten years or seventy years, but for eternity. We have been created, appointed and designed for eternity. Our life on this earth is only a parenthesis in the context of eternity, and God has programmed us for eternity. Thus Ecclesiastes 3:11 describes God placing eternity within our hearts.

But how can we understand the concept of eternity?

Eternity is not just endless time

In contemporary usage, the term 'eternity' tends to be used
to indicate an interminable length of time. A journey to the
beach with two 4-year-olds in the back of the car can seem
like eternity. Waiting for your exam results, the outcome of
an interview or a medical diagnosis can seem like eternity.
However, eternity should not be viewed only in terms of
length of time. Actually, it defines timelessness or boundless
time rather than length of time. It provides a God-lifestyle of
freedom from all that time precludes. God is eternal because
he is free from any restraints of time. Eternity provides an
extension of time in terms of its quality as well as its duration.
It will be infinitely extended time. But also, it will be boundless
time determined by the life of God as expressed in eternity in
contrast to that expressed in the confines of life on earth.

Exploring the concept of eternity is easier said than done.
There are difficulties in such a quest. The first is that it is
beyond the finite mind to understand that which is outside time
and to imagine beyond that which we know. Eternity, by definition, is beyond our current knowledge, as is the God who dwells
within it. Secondly, the Bible does not reveal a great deal about
eternity. Instead, it drops hints and encourages us to consider it,
to allow our imagination to explore it, to savour the flavour of
the life that belongs to God and to anticipate it.

Eternity is significant because of what it represents

The Bible often refers to the concept of eternity to stress the
quality of salvation for the believer. Salvation will last for
eternity (Heb 9:15), and believers are cared for by an eternally
existing God (Rom 16:26), whose power is eternal (Rom 1:20).
The Bible also uses the term to highlight the exalted nature
of God by describing him as the One who 'inhabits eternity'

(Isa 57:15). Its most common occurrence is in the context of eternal life granted to the believer (John 3:15). Although this is often viewed as describing life after death, it is more accurately understood as a life in relationship with God that commences at salvation (John 3:36), but is fully realised after death; a life in which believers can benefit from all that God makes available to them as his children.

What is most important for us is not trying to understand how it can be that God never comes to the end of his existence (and never begins it, for that matter), but rather exploring the consequences of this fact. God's eternal nature does not have the negative associations of a static, unmoved, impersonal being who is unfeeling and remote. On the contrary, he willingly experiences some aspects of our lives (Eph 4:30). His nature does not change, although he adapts himself to identify with our changeableness. He is not frozen, but full of feelings for his creation; not wooden, but aware of how we are; warm, not cold; active, not passive; present, not absent.

God is self-existent: he does not depend on anything else for his existence (Exod 3:14). No one brought him into being, neither has anyone created any framework within which he must exist. Time is the context in which some of God's purposes are achieved. He is present throughout time, though eternity is the characteristic that best defines his being (Ps 29:10). God's eternal existence means that he is steady and steadfast, and provides safety and security (Ps 90:1). His promises (Ps 102:27), his certainty and trustworthiness (Rev 1:4), his experience and wisdom are unalterable. This means that God cannot be improved upon. Every decision he makes is perfect. He has no need to reconsider or change his mind (Mal 3:6). He never gets old and he was never young. He is as he always has been and as he always will be: perfect.

Eternity represents the antithesis of this life and its negative aspects. Eternity is an era of sinlessness, joy, fulfilment and unlimited access and proximity to God. In a world of changing values and uncertainties, the fact that God is eternal assures us of his open-ended commitment to us, unaffected by the variations caused by time.

The healthier and the more accurate our perception of eternity, the more positively it will impact our lives. Many of us make a considerable investment in this life. Our time, talents and gifts are poured into this life as if it was all we had. We need to be careful that the time-bound agenda of secular society does not determine our own destinies and programmes as Christians. Other issues may be more important than those that currently occupy our lives. We need to focus on these timeless principles that are vital to our existence, or we shall end our lives having failed to concentrate on what matters centrally to us, namely God and eternity.

Eternity is what Christians have been created for

I used to fear eternity because I thought that it involved only judgement. Picture the scene: God's eyes burning into my conscience; all my friends standing around me, staring. An orchestra of frowning angels plays a slow, throbbing dirge, conducted by an angel who keeps looking at me as if I shouldn't be there. A big bass drum is beaten heavily and monotonously. Christians are marched in, heads bowed. I'm third in the queue, following Billy Graham and the Pope. 'Silence!' The books are opened and it's my turn. Oh yes, I know I'm in the Book of Life. It's the other book that troubles me – the one that measures my words, deeds and thoughts. I don't want my worst moments shouted from the housetops. I don't mind eternity; it's the first few minutes that trouble me!

Some people think of eternity as the time when normal activity ceases, to be replaced by month-long choir practices and year-long prayer meetings. Little wonder that few sermons get preached about heaven nowadays! Do many people relish that kind of heaven? Even though most Christians recognise that these pictures are caricatures of the life hereafter, the realities of eternity and the life to be enjoyed within it are still, to a large degree, unexplored mysteries.

Rather than seeking to identify details of the life to be experienced after death, it is more productive to recognise that, whatever it will be like, it is that for which believers have been created. Eternity is not the full-time whistle; it's when the fulfilment actually begins. Eternity is not the end of time; it's the start of endless time. It's not the final scene; it's not the moment of applause. Eternity is the start of the performance of our lives. Believers are ushered through this life for the purpose of eternity, destined for eternity. Eternity is not the reward for life on earth; it's not the bonus; it's the reason for our creation. Life on this earth is not the reason for our salvation; it's just the entrance porch, the waiting-room, the gateway to our destiny, which is eternity.

Life doesn't end when eternity begins; to a very significant degree, it begins. Death is the magic carpet that releases us into the glory of eternity. Eternity is the time when we shall do best the task for which we were created – endlessly exploring God. Now, we are like yachts in the harbour, ready to sail on the ocean of God's greatness, but becalmed because of our intellectual weakness and sinful tendencies. In eternity, we shall be transformed and shall endlessly discover the infinite clarity and sparkling treasures of the depths of God's glory. Eternity is not an uneventful, static and quasi-frozen state. John Baillie wrote: 'I thank Thee, O Lord, that Thou hast so set eternity within my heart that no earthly thing can ever satisfy me wholly.' Only then will all out longings be satisfied.

Eternity is a quest to be commenced in this life

We have all eternity to be intrigued by God. It will be a time to explore the innumerable mysteries of God: how he hears a leaf floating to the ground in the depths of the deepest forest and also our heartbeat; how he sees the future and the heartbreak of an orphan; how he feels the weight of the pain of his world and our tears; how he can be touched by our sorrows but not contaminated by our sin; how he could save the world and us.

God is endlessly intriguing. He cannot be completely known or understood, and he creates us for eternity to enjoy an endless exploration into him. Eternity awaits us with endless life of a quality that we can only dream of. This brief period of time on earth is a moment when he holds his breath, when he blinks his eye, but he inhabits eternity. That quest is to be commenced in this life and continued into the next.

I stand,
a lake of tranquillity stretched out before me,
serenely vast – it stills my soul.
Chameleon horizon envelopes my vision,
unique clouds blurring into forms I cannot define,
revealing glimpses of glorious colours.

Unweary rays of light melt upon my face;
magical gifts from a supernatural sun,
so pure its light, so true its intensity,
so passionate its warmth.
Such beauty inevitably reminds me of you,
the eternal Creator.

You who give orders to the morning and show dawn its
place;
you who bring forth the constellations in their seasons;
you who send lightning bolts on their way;
you who shut the sea behind doors when it bursts forth
from the womb.

You who know when the mountain goat gives birth
and watch when the foal bears her fawn.
You who give the horse its strength
and clothe his neck with a flowing mane.
You who endow the heart with wisdom

and give understanding to the mind.

You who hunt the prey for the lions
and satisfy the hunger of the lions when they crouch in
their dens.
The hawk takes flight by your wisdom
and spreads his wings towards the south.
The eagle soars at your command
and builds his nest on high.

I stand,
delighting in the majesty of my God.
So little do I comprehend of your creation.
I'm like a child with a picture book.
Angels, as bumble bees in a field of daffodils,
whisper in my ear,
and I turn to the one who's been holding my hand.
A contagious smile creeps on to your face
as we walk down the yellow-bricked path of eternity
towards my Father's Paradise.

Luke Warrington, based on Job 39

Questions for discussion

1. How can we know that we have eternal life? (John 6:47;
   Titus 1:2; 1 Pet 5:10; 1 John 2:25; 5:11)
2. How can we understand eternal life better if we think of it
   as knowing God? (John 17:3)
3. How can the fact that God is eternal make a difference to
   our sense of security? (Deut 33:27)
4. How can the idea of eternity change our lives? (Eccl 3:11)
5. What impact does the fact that God is eternal have on our
   relationship with him? (Heb 13:8)

Questions to think about

1. What impact can the fact that God is eternal have on our lives and futures?
2. In what ways is eternity more than endless time?
3. Shall we grow in knowledge in eternity?
4. What is the relationship between time and eternity?

4 He's beyond us but he beckons us

Have you ever wondered:

- whether we shall ever fully comprehend God?
- why God created humanity?
- why God gives people the opportunity to have a relationship with him?
- why God wants Christians in heaven, with him, for ever?

The answer to each of the last three questions is the same. It has to do with the fact that God wants Christians to enjoy him; to enjoy not simply a relationship with him but also to enjoy *him*. The answer to the first question is that not even eternity will be long enough to appreciate God fully, but it will provide us with the opportunity to explore God, in his presence, for ever. The seventeenth-century writer Jeremy Taylor wrote, 'A religion without mystery is a religion without God.' God is full of mystery, but he helps us feel our way to him.

Some while ago, I was wondering what I should speak about to a large group of theological students. My thoughts went like this:

'Lord, what shall I talk about?'

'Tell them about me.'

'But I don't know enough about you.'

'I know. You never will; neither will they; so journey together into me and, as you do, you will arrive at worship.'

One of the miracles of Christianity is that God, who is far beyond us, has enabled us to focus on him intimately. This opportunity to gaze upon God is to be our eternal destiny. This destiny shows why God created humanity in the first place and why he welcomes us into an active relationship with him that commences in this life. To be certain of the welcome and to discover how to develop it in this life should be our constant preoccupation as believers. The invitation that God whispers to us every day is to take pleasure in him passionately.

God is glorious

But first, it's important to remember how different God is from us. The Bible describes him as glorious. The concept of 'glory' is not easy to define. Often the Bible speaks of people seeing God's glory (Isa 6:1–3; John 1:14). It is best to understand this as becoming aware of God as he manifests himself in a particular way. The concept of glory is also associated with the kingdom of God (1 Thess 2:12).

The word 'glory' may mean splendour, majesty or magnificence. It is best used as a superlative when attempting to describe something or someone superior to all others. The Greek word used in the New Testament is *doxa*, from which the English word 'doxology' is derived. In the Greek version of the Old Testament, often used by the writers of the New Testament, this word often translates the Hebrew word *kabod*, which describes someone who has influence (Gen 45:31), riches (Gen 31:1) or power (Isa 8:7). It is used to refer to someone or something that makes an impression. God is impressive, and the term 'glory' indicates this. As the cloud that signified God's presence weighed down upon the tabernacle (Exod 40:34), the picture of God is well expressed as one who is substantially important. He has presence. He has weight, influence and authority. In this regard, the word 'glory' is best used of God. He is superior to all and the word that is used to represent his deity

('Godness') is 'glory'. What defines God most completely is that he is glorious, and in that he is unique.

To attempt to describe the supreme magnificence of God is difficult because of the limitation of language and our inability fully to comprehend his splendid majesty. This is where the word 'glory' is particularly useful, as it is our best attempt to represent something of the radiant grandeur of God. He is glorious; as such, he has no equal. Where he is, it is glorious, and he manifests himself gloriously (Exod 24:17). Charles Spurgeon, the nineteenth-century preacher, writes, 'There is nothing little in God.' Everything about him is best expressed in superlatives, for he is awesome. God is different, set apart, incomparable, unique. We may use pictures to seek to define just how uniquely excellent he is, but they all fail to do justice to his unrivalled distinctiveness.

Windows into God's glory

The biblical writers express the glory of God in superlative language and record a few incidents that paint pictures of his radiance. The best picture of God's glory is the person of Jesus, who reflects God and radiates his character. Thus, the perfect nature of Jesus reflects the peerless character of God, which cannot be improved upon.

Throughout the New Testament we catch glimpses of this glory when a bright light expresses the intensity of his magnificence. In the birth of Jesus, a star illuminated the way to him and God's glory shone around the shepherds. In his transfiguration, a bright light enveloped the disciples. In his exalted state, he dazzled the inhabitants of heaven (Rev 21:23) as he did Saul (Acts 22:11). John's vision presents him as a superior being whose presence radiates the most intense brightness imaginable (Rev 1:16). This concentration of light creates the sense of purity and distinctiveness. The miracles of Jesus also manifested his glory, revealing something of his being (John 2:11); and his ascension is encapsulated by the word 'glory' (1 Tim 3:16).

However, this glory is also seen in his death, for in that event the love of God is most clearly expressed (John 12:23). Glory is demonstrated not only in the magnificent light of God's transcendent authority, but also in the pain of darkness, when he humbles himself to take on fragile weakness. Wherever God is, there is his glory. His very existence causes him to radiate some of that which makes him impressively unique.

Believers will participate in his glory

Although, as believers, we would naturally withdraw from God because of our imperfections, he beckons us to him and invites us to explore his person. Why? The *Westminster Shorter Catechism* states that our chief purpose is to glorify God and to enjoy him for ever. This is our eternal privilege: to enjoy admiring the glorious aspects of God.

Although God's glory is what makes God unique, Paul (Rom 8:17,18) and Peter (1 Pet 5:1,4) state that believers will participate in that glory, enjoying God's presence so intimately that we shall be infused with some of his glorious characteristics. This will be partially because the new bodies that we shall receive will share some of the properties of the resurrection body of Jesus (Phil 3:21). Consequently, Paul says we shall experience 'glorious liberty' (Rom 8:21), and that God is preparing a 'weight of glory beyond all comparison' for all believers (2 Cor 4:17). The picture he paints is of a vast collection of presents, flowing from his lavish generosity, that God will bestow on believers. And if we feel unworthy of such liberty and generosity, the Spirit who lives in each of us guarantees that this will happen (Col 1:27).

An awareness of his glory leads to worship

We do not give glory to God. It already belongs to him (1 Pet 4:11). Our role is to acknowledge that he is glorious and to appreciate its significance for our own lives. When we become aware of the awesome majesty of God we shall naturally feel fear and uncertainty in the presence of such a powerful, unknowable being. But everything we know about his attitude to believers leads us to experience very different emotions, best expressed in worship.

The angels can teach us how to worship God as we increasingly appreciate his glory. Who knows God better than the angels, who live in his presence? Their worship of God is based on 'quality assessments' of him. In other words, their awareness of his character is what stimulates their worship. Seven words form the basis of their worship: 'Blessing, and glory, and wisdom, and thanksgiving, and honour, and power, and might, be unto our God for ever and ever' (Rev 7:12, Authorised Version).

The first word, 'blessing', fundamentally means 'happy'. To bless someone carries with it the idea of making that person happy. The angels are engaged in an activity that is intended to give God pleasure. In seeking to bring pleasure to God, they rehearse his attributes and his intrinsic worth, which inevitably leads them to worship him.

The result of this exploration of God should be threefold. It should result first in an increased sense of awe; secondly in changes in our emotions, our lifestyles and our readiness to follow him closer; and thirdly a recognition that this is a precursor of worship to be developed, for it will be the basis of our eternal worship. God is infinitely to be explored and therefore infinitely to be worshipped.

Though he's beyond us, he beckons to us

This is an anonymous imaginary conversation between God and a Christian that I came across some time ago:

When I said to the Lord, 'I am so short of where you want me to be,' he gently answered, 'That's OK. That's all the farther you and I can walk together.'

When I said to the Lord, 'I don't know who I am,'
he gently answered, 'That's OK. I know who you are.'

When I said to the Lord, 'I am so tired of fighting,'
he gently answered, 'That's OK. Satan is down for the count.'

When I said to the Lord, 'My mind is corrupted,'
he gently answered, 'That's OK. Use mine for a while.'

When I said to the Lord, 'I don't know how to love,'
he gently answered, 'That's OK. I will give you free lessons.'

I want to worship, Lord, but I'm not sure what to do.
Do you want me to sing a song to you? Should I sing it soft
or loud?
What would you prefer me to do?
Should I stand or sit or clap my hands? Should I raise them
high or laugh or cry?
Should I join with others or get alone,
where I can be at peace with you?

Should I sit in a church and join with the crowds
or go to the country and gaze at the clouds?
Should I praise you now for all you are, or thank you for all
that you've done?
I really want to worship you, Lord, and hear you say,
'Thank you, my son.'
But how can I worship you? Please tell me how.
What pleases you most when before you I bow?
What can I give you, since you are complete?
How can I worship while I kneel at your feet?

'Son, I don't depend on your worship;
I don't need it in the way you assume.
There are no rules for worship before I give you more room
in my heart. I don't count up the minutes you praise me.
I'm not disappointed with you.

When I call you to worship, I call you to me,
to the me that's important to you.
And when we're together in worship, you see,
it's not your praise or thanksgiving I need.
It's giving you the chance to gaze upon me.

'Take time to explore me with all of your mind;
discover how I'm mighty and awesome and kind;
hear the whisper, the King of Glory has stopped for a show.
I'm the show; you're the guest, the audience is you.
Sit down and see, come and receive.
I know you wish you could give more to me
but I'm asking you now to just come and watch me.
I expect a lot less than you think.
I give a lot more than you know.

'For I'm the one who has so much to give. There's nothing I
need now from you.
I'm the treasure, not your worship. I'm the gold, not your
praise.
I'm the pearl of greatest price, your wonder of endless days.
You're the watcher, the explorer, the child with a toy of its
dreams.
I'm the giver of glory for you.
Come, enjoy me for all I'm worth.
I'm worth it for you.'

Questions for discussion

1. Define the word 'glory'.
2. How can we see the glory of God? (John 14:8,9; Rom 1:20,21)
3. In what ways will our bodies be glorious in heaven? (1 Cor 15:42–44; Phil 3:21)

4. Which attributes of God help to stimulate worship? (Ps 29:10; 102:25–27; James 1:17; 1 John 3:20; Rev 19:11)

5. How can God's glory be manifested in times of weakness, such as the death of Jesus? (John 12:23; 2 Cor 4:9,10)

Questions to think about

1. Which characteristics of God are most important to you?

2. Which aspects of God lead you to worship him the most?

3. How can you develop your worship so as to incorporate a greater assessment of his attributes?

4. In what ways are you aware of God's glory being manifested in your life?

5 He forgives us

Have you ever wondered:

- how a holy God feels about me because I'm not holy?
- whether God will forgive me for committing the same sin again and again even though I wish I could stop?
- whether he forgives me for the sins I've forgotten about?
- whether he forgives me for the sins I didn't realise I'd committed?
- whether I need to apologise to him before he'll forgive me?

Holy Joe lives in my town. He used to carry a big Bible and dress in black with a grey tie and scruffy laced-up shoes. Sunday was his favourite day. He's different nowadays, but holy Joe still thinks he's 'holier than thou'. It all started with my new car. It rested in the church car park looking sleek and menacingly fast. Holy Joe parked his Robin Reliant next to mine and lifted his eyebrows as he watched me get out. I could read it in his eyes. My car represented extravagance: his represented holiness. Mine stood for luxury: his for necessity. He was a saint: I was a sinner. His sins were forgiven: mine were too big.

We walked together to church, sat together, sang together. He prayed – loud enough for me to hear. He prayed *at* me by asking God to help him to be holy and not squander his money. The pit he was digging for me was called guilt. I accidentally dropped my car keys down the drain on the way home and had to have a lift with holy Joe. It was clear what he was thinking: judgement for my sinful ways. We chugged to my house for the spare set of keys and chugged back. All the while, he talked of the missionaries in the steaming jungles, eating mangoes and bananas and riding bicycles.

That night holy Joe came to visit me and brought with him some of his friends. They sneaked into my house, into my bedroom and into my dreams. Joe introduced them to my sleeping mind. First, there was Anthony. He'd lived 1,900 years ago. He'd sold everything he had, ate just once a day and then only bread, salt and water. Joe reminded me of the meal I had eaten the night before. Not only had I eaten it, but also I'd enjoyed it, and the bottle of wine that went with it so well. In addition, even though my friend Neil had eaten much more than I had, Anthony still looked at me in a patronising sort of way.

Jerome then joined the happy crowd. He had spent his life in Palestine, escaping the temptations of Italy. He lived in a tiny room, but felt guilty for keeping a library of non-Christian books. Holy Joe sneaked up on me again and reminded me of the novel I was reading. 'Wouldn't God prefer you to read the Bible?' he softly whispered. I felt certain that he would, and slunk further back into the corner.

The great Augustine, champion against pagans and heresies, strolled in. I knew he was holy; he made even Joe look like a pagan. Augustine said holiness was a never-ending battle and went on to deplore the pleasures of the senses. Joe just looked at me. It was enough. The corner wasn't big enough for me as I tried to recede into its darkness. I knew that if that was a catalogue of holiness, I was certainly a sinner. Joe was right. The car would have to go, and my credit cards, and the freezer, and the tumble dryer, and the washingmachine (we could make do with a clothes line, couldn't we?), and the TV – *the TV*!

It was then that I woke up, my heart thumping, my eyes staring. I looked under the bed, but Joe wasn't there. I opened the curtains thinking I might see Augustine trotting down the road, but I didn't. I looked at the side of me, and it wasn't Mother Teresa lying there, but Judy, my wife. The birds were singing, the sun was shining, the kids were sleeping; it was Saturday. It had all been a diabolical nightmare.

And Joe? He crashed his Robin Reliant and the insurance

gave him a BMW. He avoided my eyes when I saw him in it. I gave him my best condescending grin, waved from across the car park and rushed into church ahead of him because I knew he wanted to explain. Actually, I think he likes it and that's why he thinks it's evil. Poor old holy Joe!

I'm forgiven, really

OK, so I'm a sinner – not because I may have a new car but because I don't meet up with God's standards. He is holy, and that means everything he does is perfect. He cannot make any mistakes, because he is perfect. The problem is that I am not, and when I think about God I feel my imperfection acutely. What should I do about it? Well, according to 1 John 1:8, I should acknowledge it, not deny it. John encourages his readers to accept that they are sinners but not that they're unforgivable. In 1 John 2:1,2 he reminds them and us that if we sin, Jesus takes it upon himself to speak on our behalf; he came to forgive our sins. Thus the holiness of God does not become a barrier between us and God; instead, he chooses to embrace us and welcome us as forgiven sinners who then commence the journey to holiness.

It was 9.45 on Saturday morning, 22 January. I had just returned from an elders' prayer breakfast and the house was quiet. Anna-Marie, our daughter, was in her bedroom; Luke, our son, had just returned to university and Judy was in the conservatory. I walked through the house and saw her crying on the settee. My first reaction was that she had received some sad news, but her Bible was on her lap. When I asked why she was crying she replied, 'I've just been thinking how much I've been forgiven by God.' Her reflection on this truth had moved her to tears of joy. As Christians we have been invited to explore God's forgiveness and to relax in the recognition that God has forgiven us.

The fear of taking God's forgiveness for granted is sometimes so great that we fail to take time to enjoy the fact that we have been forgiven. I get concerned that I might get blasé about sin and fall into it too easily if I concentrate on God's readiness to forgive me, so I choose not to think about it much. I am learning to recognise the fact that, though I never want to be insensitive to my sin, God encourages me to be fascinated by his forgiveness.

As believers, we regularly find ourselves making our way back to God in shame, and sometimes despair, with the same words on our lips, 'I'm sorry.' Sometimes we scarcely want to raise our heads, for we are embarrassed by what we have done. We're in good company. David, the man described as being 'after God's own heart' (see Acts 13:22), knew what it was to say sorry to God (Ps 38:18). However, God restores us because that's the amazing kind of God that he is. In addition, although we must never take him or his forgiveness for granted, it's appropriate to acknowledge it and enjoy the incredible nature of such mercy. I'm learning to recognise that it's not the act of falling in sin that's the problem – but staying down in the dust, afraid to look up. Abraham Lincoln said, 'I am not concerned that you have fallen – I am concerned that you arise.' It's important to recognise the significance of our sin and not to assume quickly that it doesn't matter. But, at the same time, wallowing in guilt and self-condemnation is not God's plan for us. He would prefer us to recognise our mistake, ask for his forgiveness and move on, determined not to fall so easily next time.

Knowing I'm forgiven helps me relax

In an article entitled 'Finding the Eye of the Storm', Craig Barnes discusses how to enjoy God's grace during the storms of life. He writes, 'When you're convinced of God's love, you're not so frightened. I don't have to succeed as a pastor: I just have to be convinced I'm forgiven by my Father ... If I know that, I'm free to enjoy being a husband and a dad and a pastor.'

Billy Graham states, 'In these days of guilt complexes, perhaps the most glorious word in the English language is "forgiveness".' Knowing I'm forgiven by God helps me relax. I'll make lots of mistakes in my life and, while I'm not indifferent to that, I know that my sins have all been forgiven and now I'm his child. The world looks different from the resurrection side of the cross. Knowing we're forgiven by God puts life in perspective. We don't realise just how forgiven we are because we don't know how much we are loved. In addition, we start this adventure of exploring God's forgiveness knowing we're never going to reach the end.

My children don't realise how much they are loved. The more they do, the more they'll be able to relax. Will they be tempted to take advantage of my readiness to forgive them? It's a risk – but you see, they're my children and I'll love them anyway. I want them to relax with me, enjoy my presence, and know they're accepted. And God's the same – only better.

Do you remember that, when Peter lacked trust in Jesus when walking on the water and thought he was going under, Jesus took him over to the other side? My sins will often cause me to go under the waters of guilt, but God is prepared to take me over to the other side of forgiveness and restoration. Peter learned the reality of this process; painful but not pointless, and ultimately productive.

Knowing I'm forgiven keeps me going

Do you remember the occasion when Elijah had let God down big time? He'd run away from Jezebel. God had used him in a remarkable way to humiliate the prophets of Baal by the miracle of fire on a drenched sacrifice. He'd fearlessly preached to the Jewish people and, with incredible courage, had told King Ahab what God thought of him. He'd ordered those prophets be put to death. He'd seen rain for the first time for three years as a result of what God did through him. Finally, God miraculously turned him into an Olympic sprinter and he ran home, overtaking Ahab's chariot on the way. He'd seen more miracles in one day than most of us see in a whole life (1 Kings 18). However, three verses later he was running scared (19:3). He failed to trust that same God and, in fear, he ran from a mere mortal.

What did God do?

God sent an angel with a miraculous breakfast in bed: freshly baked bread, still warm, a jar full of water – all within arm's reach. It sustained him for forty days. God reminded Elijah of his closeness to him, despite what he'd done. When he did speak to Elijah, he spoke in a gentle whisper and said, 'It's OK. I've got another job for you to do' (see 1 Kings 19:15).

Recognising that God forgives us provides a platform for us to proceed. God knows you'll fail before you do. It's no surprise to him when you blow it. He knows us better than we know ourselves and he's still committed to us. He's not surprised when he has to forgive us again, and again, and again.

A friend of mine felt he had let the Lord down badly, and for a long time he found it difficult to accept that God could forgive him. Eventually, he confronted his fears and explored God's forgiveness and said sorry. He summed up his experience in these words: 'I wish I'd realised how ready God was to pick me up, dust me down and start me off again.' Knowing we're forgiven because we're loved keeps us going.

Knowing I'm forgiven keeps me in awe of God

Centuries ago, a man called Anselm wrote a book called *Cur Deus Homo*. Thankfully it's been translated from the Latin! The title means *Why God became Man*, and Anselm sought to respond to this question. I have often wondered about it too. Why did God bother? What did he hope to get out of it that he didn't already have? He doesn't need our service or worship. He is completely self-sufficient, in need of nothing. Why get involved, especially when he must have known that we'd spoil his dream? What was the point, especially when achieving our salvation would cost him the life of his Son? Why did God become our Saviour?

God didn't save us because *we* were special. He saved us because *he's* special, and he wanted us to have the chance to explore just how special he is. The gift of forgiveness is his eternal prism that radiates his grace to us, and the sight and the beauty of that forgiveness are awesome. Through the lens of forgiveness, the portrait of God is unbelievable. It's what gives him the eternal 'wow' factor.

For me, confession is very important – not because it gives me an opportunity to whip myself metaphorically over all my sins, but because it gives me a chance to know his forgiveness. Confession, for me, isn't proof that I'm good at saying sorry. It's an opportunity for me to be in awe of his graciousness in forgiving me. God's forgiveness is thorough; it's final; it's a present possession; it's an experience to enjoy.

Recognising we're forgiven is the strongest impetus for us to love God. I don't love God because he's mighty or because he knows everything or because he can answer all my prayers, but because he's so lovable, so full of grace and forgiveness. His willingness to forgive demonstrates his love at its most intense. God is never concerned that he might be forgiving us too much. Worship is the inevitable result of considering such forgiveness.

Knowing I'm forgiven leads to an inevitable response

Remember, we're all different and we respond to God differently. My wife Judy responded to God's forgiveness in tears. One man, who had just completed a long term in prison, responded to God's forgiveness by shouting at the top of his voice, 'I'm saved! I'm saved! I'm saved!' My own response is to think about it, discuss it, explore it, probe it, like a little boy who has been given a tantalising present, because it seems too good to be true. I want to taste my forgiveness, like some new fruit that's juicier than all others.

The form of our response is not particularly important. What really matters is whether our response draws us deeper into God's love and to a more godly lifestyle (Rom 6:17,18). Forgiveness is for real. What's important is that we explore the reality of this gift. We don't have to look at the awfulness of our sin to recognise how much God forgives us. The devil would prefer us to remember our sin. Our Father wants us never to forget his love. Isn't that how good parents treat their children? Would you want to keep reminding your children of their mistakes, rubbing their noses in the way they've spoilt themselves? No, you want to rescue them, lift them out of their problem, sort them out, love them, forgive them, let them feel they're forgiven, let them be part of you again. Jesus came to earth not simply to tell us that he was ready to forgive, but actually to forgive.

Do you remember the paralysed person whose friends brought him to Jesus for healing? The first thing Jesus did was to forgive him for all his sins (Matt 9:2). It wasn't that his sin had caused his paralysis; it was that sin was his biggest problem, the one that Jesus wanted to sort out first. He could still get to heaven as a paralytic, but not if his sins remained unforgiven. But do you notice there is no record that he repented or even acknowledged his sins? Jesus had come to forgive. Imagine if he had said, 'Wait, Jesus, I haven't said sorry yet. Don't forgive me until I've repented.' Too late! Jesus had already forgiven him. That's the quality of Jesus' forgiveness. Jesus wasn't going to wait. He forgave the man before he had had a chance to ask for forgiveness. When John tells us, 'If we confess our sins, he is faithful and just and will forgive us' (1 John 1:9), he is describing not so much a process as the inevitability of forgiveness for those who confess their sins to God.

Forgiveness is an adventure in understanding how to say 'Thank you' to God; an opportunity to pursue a kind of shyness that says, 'Can it really be true? Can I really be that forgiven? Do you mind if I ask you again about my forgiveness? Can I say I'm forgiven, really, for good; for ever?'

Forgiveness: an opportunity to hear God whisper into my mind the words of Hosea 11:7,8, 'How can I give you up' even if you 'are determined to turn from me'? These words scare me because they express a love I don't understand. I am left in awe of a Father who can forgive so much for so little in return and for ever. I may cry, laugh, shout, sing – but I shall always want to bow before such a God.

Learn to explore your forgiveness; celebrate it; feel it; and never forget that it's God's greatest gift to you.

Can it be that
my sins of yesterday are forgiven,
my sins of today have been forgiven,
my sins of tomorrow will be forgiven?

Can it be that
God has welcomed me as his child?

Can it be that
I am forgivable,
I am acceptable,
I am accepted,
I am forgiven?
Yes,
even me?

But my sin looms like a wall before my eyes.
It blocks my sight of God;
it blots my life;
it bruises my best intentions;
it breezes its way into my life
again
  and again
   and again;
it breaks my heart.

Before my burning bush,
I bow my head.

Words drift into my mind.

'Your sins of yesterday are forgiven;
your sins of today have been forgiven;
your sins of tomorrow will be forgiven.
It is certain;
it has been decided by me, your God.
I have welcomed you as my child.

'Therefore,
you are forgivable,
you are acceptable,
you are accepted,
you are forgiven.

'Yes,
especially you.'

Questions for discussion

1. Does God forgive our sins if we've forgotten to apologise to him? (Ps 130:3,4)

2. Does God forgive sins that we commit again and again when we're sorry that we have done so? (Ps 103:10–12; Neh 9:17)

3. Is there any sin too serious for God to forgive? (1 Kings 8:50; Jer 33:8; Luke 23:34)

4. Does God forgive deliberate sins as readily as accidental sins if we are sorry? (Ps 32:5; 1 John 1:9)

5. Will God still punish us even though he has forgiven us? (Isa 6:7)

Questions to think about

1. If we died before we had confessed some sins to God, would he still forgive us?

2. Does God forgive the sins that we're not aware of having committed?

3. Why is 'blasphemy against the Spirit' (Matt 12:31) viewed as unforgivable?

4. Does God forgive us because we're his children or because we ask him to?

6 He's adopted us

Have you ever wondered:

- what it means to be a child of God?
- why Paul uses the image of adoption?
- how God can adopt anyone?
- why God adopts anyone?

Socrates said, 'Wisdom begins in wonder.' When I think about God and reflect that I can call him Father, I often wonder, 'Why?' Why did he choose to be my Father? Calling him God or King would have made more sense, but to call him by such a personal term as Father seems a luxury I don't deserve.

Of course, too many people have a poor experience of their fathers in childhood. However, our failure to appreciate God's fatherhood adequately is due not so much to that experience as to a limited awareness of the perfection of his fatherhood. The Bible offers analogies from human fatherhood, but only as a springboard to explore the much more remarkable aspects of God's fatherhood. God does not have natural children, since everyone has been created by him; but the concept of *adoption* helps us to discover the incredible fatherliness of God.

Adoption of a child is one of the oldest expressions of social harmony and love, dating back to the ancient Babylonian and Egyptian empires. Every reference to adoption in the New Testament is by Paul, and most of them refer to Christians. The question to be explored is; why did Paul choose to use this term to describe the relationship between God and his people? One answer is that 'adoption' describes the greatest privilege available to humanity, more significant even than salvation itself.

Adoption before the time of Jesus

Central to the act of adoption was the privileged position of the one adopted and also the significance of the one choosing to adopt. Two of the most celebrated people in the Old Testament had one thing in common. Moses, who rescued the Jewish people from slavery in Egypt, and Esther, who rescued them from being massacred by their enemies, were both adopted. The activities of both are celebrated annually in the feasts of Passover and Purim respectively. Two people with initially limited prospects fulfilled great objectives because they were adopted. Being adopted offers people the chance to achieve their full potential.

Taken from obscurity as just one group of people out of many, the Jews were adopted by God (Rom 9:4). God now became their Father and provider. They would be granted the privilege of knowing him as well as being known by him. No group other than the Jews was ever granted this privilege. When Paul wanted to describe God's relationship with Christians, he chose to use the same word used for the adoption of the Jews. But he extended its meaning to reflect the relationship that Christians have with God, which exceeds even that enjoyed by the Jews in the Old Testament.

Adoption in the time of Jesus

There is no evidence that the Israelites practised adoption in the Old Testament. All its references to adoption are to non-Hebrew people. Not surprisingly, therefore, John and Peter, writing to Jews, use the image of sonship, not adoption, to describe the Christian's relationship with God. Only Paul, writing to Gentiles, uses the term 'adoption'. Not only do the Old Testament pictures of God adopting the people of Israel parallel the way God has rescued unbelievers and transferred them into his family, but adoption in the non-Jewish world of the time sheds further light on what God has done for us. Paul's readers, aware of the custom, would understand what Paul was getting at. What then did adoption involve?

Adopted people enjoy an exalted relationship with a father, experienced by no one else but natural-born sons, and shared equally with them. Adoption becomes the basis for knowing God (Gal 4:4–9). The adopted child can call God 'Abba, Father' (Rom 8:15). The word *abba* means 'father', and was the word Jewish children used to address their fathers. Only two children in the world can refer to me as their father: Luke and Anna-Marie. It is a relationship that only they can enjoy with me; they are my children and I am their father. There is a special exclusiveness about this bond. This is what makes adoption even more remarkable than salvation. It is one thing for God to forgive us our sins; it is another for him to welcome us as members of his family. It is true that before we can become members of his family we have to be forgiven, but being forgiven does not inevitably entail being allowed to be his children.

When we became Christians, it was because our sins were forgiven. That is a gracious gift, far greater than we deserved. But God went beyond that and welcomed us into his family; not just for the afternoon, dressed in our best clothes, but for eternity; not just to be shown around as if exploring a historical mansion, but to be ushered into the guest bedroom and given the key to the front door; not to function as servants and domestics, but to be sons and daughters (Gal 4:7); not as fee-paying visitors, but as valued friends (John 15:15). If we are to call God Father we need to feel confident with him, and God adopts us to make sure we do.

Adopted people are released from previous relationships and welcomed into a new family. Children are not just adopted for Christmas and then sent back to the desert of loneliness; it's a lifetime choice, and the process leading to it is carefully controlled. Christians have not been conscripted into an army or marched into a monastery; we have not been forced into a fraternity but welcomed into a family. Heaven is where friends are reunited for ever.

An adopted person becomes an heir of the father who adopts him or her and generally receives a new name. As heirs, adopted children have every right to be confident in the presence of their father. They don't have to beg permission to see him or book an appointment.

Adoption is motivated by love (Eph 1:5), not by the hope of reward or service. Adopted children are chosen. They cannot choose who adopts them. A Roman would sometimes adopt an heir if he needed a servant or slave, so it was not common for young children to be adopted. Alternatively, a man who needed an heir to carry on the family name might adopt a son. In either case the adoption was primarily for the benefit of the adoptive father. God is different. He adopts us not because he needs us. Rather, he volunteers to love us and chooses to adopt us because of it.

Adopted people are legally protected in their new relation-ship. God sees us when we're at our worst, when we don't know he's even looking at us; then he adopts us even before we've smartened up, and binds himself to that adoption by coming to live in us and improving us from the inside out (Rom 8:16,17). The Spirit who was given to us when we became Christians is the eternal evidence that our adoption is certain; he is a water-tight guarantee that our adoption is irrevocable, immediate and eternal (Eph 1:13,14). Adoption unlocks God's resources for the person adopted but cannot itself be unlocked; there is no key.

Adoption results in God making himself vulnerable; he can be hurt and even rejected by his children. Fatherhood brings pleasure but also potential pain. The pleasure parents take in the first steps of their baby contrasts with the pain of those who see their child taking the first steps towards rebellion. Children sharing smiles with their parents bring pleasure; children who slam the door, refuse to do as they are asked or shout expletives cause their parents pain. Parents allow themselves to be vulnerable because they love their children more than their children know. God does the same. The question remains: 'Why?' Heaven doesn't need to be repopulated. But the God who is joy willingly adds potential pain to his untroubled existence as part of the package of adoption.

Adoption means that the resources of God the Father are made available to his adopted children. Picture the scene. The earth is scorched, the land is flat and barren as far as the eye can see. The wind whistles around you. You step on a twig, and the sound of its crack lingers in the air. The blown sand drifts against ruined walls and settles there. Your home and future are buried beneath it. Life has retreated from this desolation.

Where are the laughing children, the farmyard animals, the flocks of sheep on the hills, the footprints in the sand? There's nothing but a few lonely trees, crumbling walls, dashed dreams and hollow hopes. The flocks have gone; the people are dead or exiled; the city that once was Jerusalem has been destroyed and the land lies close to death; the crown of Israel has been robbed of its precious stones. Numbness fills the few who escaped the carnage and, as they brood over their troubles, they begin to sense despair.

This is a time when the people need someone to cling to, a big brother, a father who can soothe their fears and tell them everything will be all right. God sends a young man with limited powers but a life changing promise. The prophet Jeremiah introduced a new name for God that the people needed to hear: 'the LORD our Righteousness' (Jer 33:16). God's promise to the people through Jeremiah was that he was on their side. Although the situation was desperate and the forces against them were frightening and deadly, someone whose power was unimaginable was closer to them than the sand that clung to their clothes. His role was to make right what had been wrecked, to restore what had been ruined, to vindicate the victims and to be a father to the frightened. The king who reigned in Jeremiah's time was Zedekiah (whose name means 'The LORD is my righteousness/vindication'). Jeremiah's message was that, when the people trusted this king whose name signified certainty and assurance, he failed them. That would not happen with God. His dedication to his children is unshakeable.

There are times in the lives of all of us when dreams become disasters and hopes are torn and shredded, left to blow in the wind that always seems to be against us, bringing with it cold fears and stinging pain. But the promise remains the same, for although we may be children newly added to the family, the Father does not change (Mal 3:6). Even though others hurt us, he remains the Father who views each of his children as priceless and who cares for them sensitively; and all the bills for these services are sent to his account.

Conclusion

When God adopts us as his children we become co-heirs with Christ and share in his glory (Rom 8:17). Of course, adopted children have responsibilities as well as privileges in their new families. Matthew says that God's children are to love those who are unfriendly or hurtful (5:44). Similarly, because we are children of God, he chooses to improve us, and sometimes that can be painful (Heb 12:5–11). Chasing after sin will result in chastening by God. He does this because we matter to him, not because he's enraged by our behaviour and determined to punish us so that we cower in fear. He punishes us as a good father punishes his child, for whom he would willingly sacrifice his life. He wants his children to be the best they can be, and he helps them in that direction because he loves them (Rev 3:19).

Becoming a child of God stills sounds too good to be true, but it *is* true. Adopted children don't change to look like their father, but Christians do. That's because of the Spirit, one of whose roles is to work on our characters, improving us and helping us to change. This proactive commitment is based on his dedication to our development as children of God. Explore what it means to be a son or daughter of God now, and then imagine what it will be like in heaven. Just as a baby doesn't appreciate what it will achieve as a child, so our future too is unimaginable.

Before time's fabric was begun,
before anything was said or done,
you know you've always been the only one.

In Paradise full, fresh, man dwelt with you,
among bluebird songs, nature's palette true
till an inverse 'son'rise. With pride he withdrew.

At so many 'cross'roads have you yearned for him,
tear-stricken eyes felt adoration grow dim,
each generation, consecration more thin.

Here I exist, sliding into the mould,
another deserter, heart hanging old,
the worst of all brothers, my rationale cold.

I didn't know you when you offered to me
the sole way to freedom, a misshapen tree;
by your spear-torn side, life for eternity.

Can such blood-blind eyes receive grace and see?
Your precious Son, he more than died for me,
his executioner, at Calvary.

The wilful slayer of the Servant King
has been shown forgiveness and welcomed within,
a choir robe given as heaven's angels sing.

Like the dazzling sun, so bright, shining high,
eternal gold in a sapphire sky,
your holy light shames me as I stand by.

But then I'm brought to life by sun-beam love.
Rainbow hope rises like a star-bound dove.
How can I say just what you mean to me?

And when I offer up the best of me,
it's a poor exchange for the perfect Three.
My heart is warmed with joy – thermals from thee.

So will you please accept my tears
and love away my shame and fears?
Lord, come and take me by the hand;
please lead me to the Promised Land.
For I just want to smile at you,
for all the good things that you do.

And finally now the time has come,
when everything's been said and done.
You know you're still the only one
for me.

Luke Warrington

Questions for discussion

1. How do we know that we have been adopted by God as his children? (John 1:12; 1 John 3:1,2)

2. How does being adopted as God's children help us in our relationship with God? (Matt 6:9; Heb 12:5–10)

3. How does the fact that we are adopted by God make a difference to our sense of security? (Rom 8:14–17,23)

4. How can the fact that we are God's adopted children affect our relationship with other believers? (Eph 5:1,2; 1 Tim 5:1,2)

5. How does the term 'Abba, Father' help us in prayer? (Rom 8:15; Gal 4:5)

Questions to think about

1. What impact does the fact that we are adopted as sons and daughters of God have on our lives and futures?
2. What differences can we make in our lives in order to be more like God, our Father?
3. Why did God choose to adopt us as his children?
4. Identify three practical ways in which knowing we are God's adopted children can affect our relationships with other Christians.

7 He's all-powerful and we're not

Have you ever wondered:

- whether God could ever lose a battle?
- if God is all-powerful, why life is so unfair?
- if God is all-powerful, why I am so weak?
- how much less powerful than God the devil is?

How big is your God?

Many years ago, JB Phillips wrote a book entitled *Your God is Too Small*. In a world that believes its own press about its own accomplishments, we are in danger of losing sight of the greatness of God, whose unique might, ingenuity and authority are awesome. The Bible is clear that God is all-powerful. It describes him as sitting above the earth, the people like grasshoppers, people-powers being as nothing in comparison to his power (Isa 40:22). The nations are described as drops in a bucket, dust on a set of scales (Isa 40:15). But these expressions of God's power sometimes fall flat because they do not seem to be borne out in reality in this world and in our lives. We can even be tempted to think that if we had God's power we would make some changes, which raises the question, 'Why doesn't he?'

Why doesn't God do what we expect?

The village of Corozalito is filled every day with the screeching of colourful parrots, the call of howler monkeys and the bustle of the 94 people who live there, deep in the heart of the Columbian jungle. Most of them are Christians, due to the witness of an uneducated farmer named Victor. Victor came from a profligate background, operating a brothel, living with three women simultaneously while being addicted to alcohol. But he became a Christian and led his whole family to the Lord, followed by most of his village. From Corozalito he began to reach out to the surrounding villages, establishing groups of believers wherever he went, travelling by horseback, dugout canoe and on foot. Over about 15 years Victor led hundreds of people to Christ, as a result of which dozens of churches sprang up in Northern Columbia. The power of God was clearly seen.

Then he heard of an Indian tribe deep in the jungles of the Choco region, near the border with Panama, who had never heard of the name of Jesus. He decided to move there. In order to learn their language he lived with them, hacking a small farm out of the jungle in order to survive. Fifteen years later, at a conference for Christians in one of the bigger cities, he was with friends who wanted to know what progress had been made. His reply was startling. Although he had been there for 15 years, the Indians were so nomadic and volatile that no church had yet been established. After seeing dozens of churches established during the first 15 years of his ministry, it was almost inconceivable to see the opposite result in the second 15 years. Success and failure? Victory and defeat? The sight of God's blessing and God's turning away? The presence and absence of God's power? We shall see Victor's response later.

In my first week as a minister pioneering a church in Bootle, Merseyside, a young Christian asked me to pray for his young wife, who was dying of cancer. I visited her with my wife Judy and we prayed that her ravaged body would be restored to health by God's power. But a few days later she died. Her desperate husband rang me to tell me the sad news and asked me to come and pray for her again. He had read that Jesus had raised people from the dead and wanted me to ask him to do it again. Of course, God *could* do it again; the question was whether he *would*. An aspect of God's character that needed to be considered alongside his power was his *will*. The distraught husband's question was, 'Why *wouldn't* he restore her?'

In order to answer that question and understand Victor's experience, one needs to revisit the scene where God's power is most clearly married with his wisdom. At the end of his life, Jesus cried out, 'It is finished' (John 19:30). So his mission must have succeeded. To nearly everyone watching, however, it looked as if he had failed, because he had died. God did not seem to be manifesting his power, intruding in a cataclysmic manner or mightily breaking into the desperate weakness and ignominy of death. Yet in the weakness of death new life was born. Jesus' death looked like a pathetic failure, but it was the climax of his perfect obedience to God's wisdom. Success was achieved in the midst of apparent failure .

The fact is that God operates by a strategy different from that which we might prefer. It is not power that determines his activity, but wisdom. When we see a problem and have the resources to deal with it, we often do so decisively, quickly, energetically and powerfully. But God's priority is seldom to effect change by the use of power. He has another agenda and operates his divine strategy to achieve it. His power is always linked to his priorities. He functions not with red-hot, raw energy, but with careful, unruffled authority.

What should we do when God doesn't do what we think he should?

When we don't see God working as we think he should, we often get confused and worried. Our logic tells us God can do anything, so when there's a problem he doesn't solve, or a prayer he doesn't answer in the way we asked, or guidance he doesn't clarify, we assume we're to blame or the devil's too strong. Perhaps we think:

- We need to do more to get God to release his power
- We should pray or fast more to see the answer to prayer
- It must be something in our character that's holding him back
- Personal sin must be clogging the channel of power from God to us
- The devil is stopping God doing what he wants to do
- God loves us less than he loves others

Most of the time, none of these is relevant. It's just that our conclusions as to how to resolve the situation are often not the same as his. When Paul wrote to the church in Ephesus, where he had spent three years as their first pastor, he introduced his letter by reminding them that God achieves everything 'in conformity with the purpose of his will' (Eph 1:11). This was important for the Ephesians because they were aware of other forces that would attempt to destabilise them. At the time, Ephesus was one of the most important occult centres of the Roman Empire. Magical charms known as 'Ephesian letters' were bought by many visitors who sought protection on long journeys or to have their wishes granted. It was in Ephesus that sorcerers' possessions were burnt on a bonfire after their owners became Christians. They knew the power of the supernatural and could harness it. Paul's message to them was not just that God had greater power but that his power was demonstrated in harmony with his will. And since God always acts perfectly his power is never arbitrary. It does not control his actions. It is not the central part of his character. His perfection is. His power is always perfectly manifested.

Similarly, there is no danger that the devil might stop God doing what he wants to do. The devil is not a competitor to God, nor is he a dark force that comes close to winning the war. He was always only a creation of God, an angel who thought he could replace God. At the moment of his rebellion he was defeated. His demise was affirmed by Jesus in his death and resurrection, and his destiny had been determined by God before he was created.

Likewise, there is no danger of God loving us less than he loves other Christians and thus responding to our situations with less care than he does to others. At this moment, God loves us as much as he will do in a million years' time. His love for us is based not on our performance as Christians but on our position as children of God.

God has power, but priorities too

When Peter searched for Jesus early one morning and told him that a crowd of people were looking for him, Jesus went away to a different location. His priority was not to heal people just then. At that moment, his priority was prayer (Mark 1:35–38). When Jesus went to the pool of Bethesda in Jerusalem, he healed only one man, who didn't even ask to be healed. Of course, he had sufficient power to heal them all; but only one man was chosen, a man who didn't even know who Jesus was. His priority was not to release his healing power but to present himself as a Saviour worthy of their trust (John 5).

When Jesus heard that his friend Lazarus was sick, John records that Jesus stayed in Jerusalem for two more days. By this time Lazarus had died (John 11:1–6,14,15. Jesus' itinerary was determined not by his power to perform but by the priority of following his Father's agenda. That's why he didn't obliterate the devil and all his demons in one demonstration of power at the commencement of his ministry. That's why he didn't make it easier for the people to accept him by devastating the Roman occupying forces from the land. That's why he didn't step down from the cross and unleash his power against those who had put him there. His power is best demonstrated in weakness because that's the way God chooses it to be.

We have questions: God has reasons

God's logic is often very different from our own, and we can too easily assume that our conclusions, based on our logic, are right. Often they are not. Our role is to trust God. Elisabeth Elliot was the wife of one of five young American missionaries who went to the Amazon jungle to share the gospel for the first time with the Auca Indians. On 11 January 1956, after the missionaries had failed to radio their families for five days and two bodies had been seen floating in the water, she wrote these words, knowing that her three young children would probably not see their father again this side of heaven: 'I have no idea what I will do if Jim is dead, but the Lord knows and I am at rest. We hope for final word tomorrow and trust our loving Father who never wastes anything.' After it was confirmed that her husband Jim and his colleagues had been killed by the people they had gone to save, she wrote, 'God knows what he is doing and he is not under any obligation to make us any explanations.'

Sometimes, there are no answers to our problems. Take Job. He lost everything. Carnage visited the greatest man in the East, devastating him and nearly destroying him. His seven sons and three daughters were cruelly snatched from him and Job began to endure his darkest hour. But the end of the story records that Job had seven more sons and three more daughters, who were the most beautiful girls in the land. So it all worked out for the good in the end. There's your answer!

But *was* that an answer? Was that enough to silence the questions in Job's mind? Was that sufficient to compensate for the pain of the loss of his children? God appears to allow a man to be robbed of his precious children and then simply replace them with others by way of compensation. Is that picture accurate and helpful? Job was fully aware that God had unimaginable resources of power at his disposal. But even after the story had ended Job didn't seem to know why God hadn't responded in power to stop the path of pain before it had begun (42:11). What we do know is that, in the context of his own powerlessness and God's non-use of his power, Job trusted God. Not easy, but he did.

The eternal future may unlock the reasons for our present sufferings. The answer is not that God cannot help, or that he is unaware of our situation, or that he doesn't love us. The answer lies in his priorities, which are often beyond our understanding. Of course, accepting this demands faith on our part. It's helpful to remember what God said through Isaiah to the Jews who were struggling to work out what was happening to them in exile: 'my thoughts are not your thoughts, neither are your ways my ways' (Isa 55:8). What we do know is that his ways are fair (Deut 32:4), right (Hos 14:9) and holy (Ps 77:13), even though we may not understand the reasoning behind them. We can commit our ways to God (Ps 37:5) because nothing happens to us that his power could not change if it was not in his perfect plan.

God's power is for overcoming life's problems, not for escaping them

Pedrilo was a feared member of one of the most violent gangs in Manila, the capital of the Philippines – the Sigue Sigue gang. Now, he is a Christian and a leader in the largest church in Smokey Mountain, the name of Manila's biggest rubbish dump. Twenty thousand people live there, their only income earned from selling whatever they can scavenge from the trash discarded by others. God has changed Pedrilo's life except in one respect, found in the name of his former gang. 'Sigue, sigue' means 'Keep going, keep going.' Life is a struggle at times; occasionally, it's an endurance test. But our role is to keep going because we have a destination, a hope and a future. We keep going in order to arrive, to reach the finishing-mark, to complete God's agenda for us, to achieve our eternal destination: the powerful presence of God.

God's power is awesome. But his role isn't always to make the mountains melt, but to make them manageable; not always to make the desert disappear, the darkness depart or the fog fade away, but to keep us, care for us and carry us through, enabling us to grow in the process. Against the forces of the evil foe, the finger of God is enough to keep us safe. When I think he's removed his finger from my life, I'm wrong. I may not know all the answers, but I am learning to trust the one who has set the agenda.

He holds the foe as he tries to push in
with an empty heart and malicious grin.
He cups his hand and shelters me there
in a cradle for him and me to share.

> *And the enemy writhes in anger and pain;*
> *desperate to unleash his evil and stain*
> *my peace with a blot of fear,*
> *to take my smile and smudge it with tears,*
> *to take my calm, my innocent joy*
> *and shake me and hurt me*
> *like an old, worthless toy.*

But there's someone between us and he can't get in.
Although he'll pretend he's a powerful king,
he's simply a bully, a thief and a fraud;
we look at him calmly
through the fingers of God
for ever
folded
around
me.

Questions for discussion

1. What powerful acts has God done in your life? (Rom 1:16; 5:1; Col 1:10,11; 2 Pet 1:3)

2. How can we access some of God's power? (Rom 1:16; Eph 1:18,19; 3:16; 6:10,11)

3. How can the fact that God is all-powerful make a difference to our sense of security? (Rom 15:13; Phil 3:10,21)

4. How is God's power manifested in the world? (Jer 10:12; Col 2:10)

5. Why does God choose to manifest his power in our weakness? (2 Cor 4:7; 12:9; 13:4)

Questions to think about

1. What is the difference between God's power and his authority, and which is more important?

2. How can you see God's power manifesting itself in your own weakness?

3. How can you help others recognise God's power when they feel powerless?

4. What would have been the result if Jesus had exercised his power and stepped down from the cross?

8 He's holy and we're accountable

Have you ever wondered:

- whether God could ever sin?
- whether God could make a mistake?
- whether God can make us holy?
- what it means to say that God is holy?

When we refer to God as being holy, it doesn't simply mean that he has never sinned or made a mistake. It does not simply refer to the fact that he is perfect and that everything he does is flawless. It's much more significant than that. God is not just the one who has never sinned, broken the law or had to say sorry. He's more remarkable than that, much more.

He's different

The fundamental meaning of the Greek word regularly translated 'holy' describes God more completely. It means 'set apart', 'different'. It's not that God is unusual, but that he is unique; he's not just out of the ordinary but one of a kind. That's what it means when he is defined as being holy. Isaiah 40:25 says, 'To whom will you compare me? Or who is my equal? says the Holy One.' Sinlessness is just part of what makes him different, but he is much more than sinless. He is set apart from anything anyone can imagine, unequalled, incomparable, irreplaceable. He's holy.

One of the reasons God is so different is that he cannot improve himself or be improved; he can't get better or worse; he can't be developed or refined; he's already ideal, and always has been and always will be. It's a rare person who is satisfied with his or her workmanship whether as a composer, author, painter, craftsman or musician. But people are even less prepared to acknowledge that they have achieved perfection in their art when a superior authority examines their work. They may have done the best they could, but they will acknowledge that it is not the best that could be achieved. But when God designs, creates or achieves anything, it is simply the best that it could be. It is not just that he has nothing equally good to compare it with; he compares it with his character, which is perfect. Everything that flows from him is flawless. He's holy. He's different.

He's definitely different

Joshua describes God as being holy because he protects his people (Josh 24:19). Joshua lived in a world where the gods were worshipped not because of their faithfulness to their subjects but because they were feared. God is different.

Samuel describes God as being holy because he is a rock (1 Sam 2:2). Unlike other so-called gods, God is dependable, safe, unshakeable and trustworthy. He's different.

Isaiah describes God as being holy because he is righteous (Isa 5:16). He doesn't make mistakes; he never worries whether he's made the right choice; he never needs to change his plans; he doesn't need an eraser. God is always right. He's different.

The same prophet also describes God as being holy because he's almighty (Isa 6:3). It's not just that he's powerful; he's all-powerful; not just that he's strong, or even very strong, but that strength resides in him. The authority of the most authoritative empire, the power of the most powerful bomb, the influence of the most influential person, the dominance of time over our lives are all but whispers in the wind of God's strength. The most powerful force is a fragile leaf blown by the breeze when compared to God. He is supreme. He's different.

For Isaiah, one dimension of God's holiness is that he redeems his people (Isa 43:14). This is something else that emphasises how different God is. When people angered the gods they expected nothing but punishment. Sickness, suffering, storms and even death were the shadows that stalked the ancient world, sent by the gods when the people upset them. But God is different because he made the first move to restore the relationship with himself that people had broken. He did not inflict malicious punishment but showed merciful patience at cost to himself. He buys us back. He's different.

He calls us to be holy

One of the most frequent commands of God to his people is to be holy because he is holy (Lev 11:45; 20:26; 1 Pet 1:16). If we think this simply means that we should be sinless, we are in for some worrying times. We may feel that God is asking us to do the impossible, since we cannot be sinless until we are in heaven (1 John 1:8). We may feel further aggrieved because we know that God knows we cannot be sinless until we get to heaven; so why does he tell us that we should be? Perhaps God is encouraging us to raise the standards of our lifestyles so that they reflect the character of Jesus. More fundamentally, however, he is asking us to recognise that he has set us apart for himself and to consecrate ourselves in practical ways to that mission. Moses explains that to be holy means to be consecrated to God (Lev 20:7), to acknowledge daily that he controls our actions, thoughts and words.

To be holy means to be set apart for God

When the word 'holy' is used in the Bible, it regularly means 'set apart for God'. Holy fruit (Lev 19:24) isn't fruit that has no bugs but fruit that has been set apart as an offering to God. The priests are called holy (Lev 21:7) not because they do not sin but because they are consecrated to God. A holy field (Lev 27:21), holy ground (Josh 5:15), a holy temple (Ps 64:5) and a holy mountain (Ps 99:9) are not uncontaminated by sin but consecrated to the service of God.

Similarly, when Paul speaks to the Christians in Corinth, he describes them as being a holy temple (1 Cor 3:17). He doesn't mean they're sinless or even good Christians. In fact, many of them were battling with a variety of sinful tendencies and habits. He is reminding them of their position as people set apart by God for a personal relationship with him and to be his messengers. That's the meaning of the word 'saint'; in the Greek it is related to the word for 'holy', and describes a person who has been set apart, by God, for God. It is a mark not of sinlessness or superiority but of sole ownership and consecration. It's not a cause for pride in what we have done but a challenge to pursue whatever God wants us to do. It's not a sign that we have arrived but a reminder that God has arrived in us.

To be holy means that we belong to God

When God described the Jewish nation as 'holy' (Exod 19:6), he was saying that he owned them. No longer were they owned by the Egyptians; now they were owned by God. Because of this, God told them, he had carried them 'on eagles' wings' (19:4). This is the kind of care that goes with the package of being under heavenly management.

Of course, there are personal implications of this new ownership: responsibilities as well as rights, prohibitions as well as privileges. In a list of guidelines for behaviour written for the Christians in Ephesus (4:17 – 6:9), Paul gives them the fundamental reason why God adopted them. In 4:30, he reminds them that sin grieves the Spirit of God, who is described as holy and the one who is committed to their salvation. This is the only time Paul describes the Spirit as 'the Holy Spirit of God' – a graphic reminder of the Spirit's status. Paul recommends his readers to consider how humiliating it would be to embarrass this Spirit by letting him down and thereby bringing his reputation as a guarantor (someone who presents them positively before God) into disrepute. It would be the height of ingratitude for people to hurt a Person who was doing this for them. Belonging to a holy God has strings attached. If we're not serious about being holy, God feels sad. It's a sobering thought that mortals can cause the immortal God to feel sorrow.

To be holy means to be different

The final reference to being holy in the Bible is in Revelation 22:11. People who are holy are contrasted with people who do wrong and compared with people who do right. Holy people are those who are trying to be better, to stamp out sin, to be thoughtful, not thoughtless, to be sensitive, not indifferent, to be as they ought to be, not as they are or were. Such people are different and holy. To be holy is thus not simply a destination but a daily process of deciding to be different.

A friend of mine has a Highland terrier, a pure white pedigree champion. She keeps it in pristine condition, bathing it regularly so that its white fur is spotless. On a winter's day after it had snowed all night, she looked out of her bedroom window on to the garden below and saw a dog run across the lawn leaving pawprints in the fresh snow. She could not understand how the dirty dog had strayed into her garden, and asked her husband to chase it away. 'But it's *your* dog!' he said. The animal that normally looked so clean and white seemed dirty compared with the sparkling snow. Our task is not to compare our lives with those of others or with our own best intentions, but with God. Aiming for his holiness is not a burden but a benchmark; meant not to inspire guilt but to encourage us to receive his grace to go forward. He has already set us apart; now he motivates us on.

How to be different

We cannot become like God quickly; it is a lifetime process, and even at the end of our lives, we shall still not have achieved our target completely. I am discovering a number of principles in this lifestyle of development.

The first priority is to *set small targets*. Rather than deciding to read the whole Bible in a month, read a chapter a day. Instead of planning an hour a day in prayer, commit to ten minutes. Don't plan to memorise a verse of Scripture every day, try one a week. Just as a golfer doesn't expect to hit a ball from the tee into the hole, so we need to be realistic in setting achievable goals.

A second principle is: *don't try to achieve too many targets at one time*. Imagine trying to keep table-tennis balls under water using only one hand. Keeping two under is not too difficult, but it gets progressively more difficult the more balls you add. Sometimes, we get into difficulties because, in our enthusiasm to be better, we try to do too much too quickly and end up failing in most attempts. It's better to be thoughtful in the choice of targets and realistic in deciding what can be achieved.

The final principle is to *set a time in which to achieve the goals*. This allows you to choose various tasks, giving you the opportunity to progress in different aspects of your life. It also helps you keep a check on how you have progressed in the time allocated. It is more important to see that you have moved forward than to worry about having missed the target if you don't achieve it in the time set. One of the practices that I regularly undertake with some friends is for each of us to set a target relating to an aspect of our growth as Christians, write it down, place the paper in an envelope and seal it with wax. Then, together, we open our envelopes six months later, and, if it's appropriate, we share how we have done. It's a practical and accountable way of trying to follow the example of Jesus and to fulfil God's desire for us to be holy as he is.

A sculptor was once asked when he would be finishing the sculpture he was working on. He stopped filing and scraping,

and as he polished the piece he said, 'I'll never finish it. I just
keep refining it until they come and take it away.' We shall
never finish refining our characters, and God doesn't expect us
to. Our role is to set a strategy for change and stay in touch with
the Spirit to achieve it, little by little, until he comes to take us
away.

There was no need for it, no reason.
No one knew why or dared to ask.
Who could? Maybe somebody should have
but nobody did ... and the plan went ahead.
There was no thread of meaning, no purpose.
Why not leave things alone instead?
He simply shook his head.
Everything was perfect before he did.
Nothing stirred the peace that reigned supreme.
But he went ahead and the world was spoilt.
All that he'd done was blown away
like fragile leaves on a stormy day.
The gold had turned to grey;
someone would have to pay
to right the wrong,
to change the darkness into day.

The Sun would have to shine again.
He simply said he would.

Why did he do it?
Why soil his hands?
I simply cannot understand
why he should stoop to create man.

Lord, I am a sinner whom you've made free.
I marvel at your love for me
that welcomes me in your family.
You're unique in all you are
and I want to be different for you.

Help me to be pure and holy and clean;
let Jesus be seen in me.

Questions for discussion

1. Since God is holy, how can we feel comfortable in his
   family? (Rom 8:1,34–39; 1 John 1:9)
2. What characteristics come to mind when you think of God
   as holy? (Exod 19:3; 1 Sam 2:2; Ps 77:13; Isa 5:16; 8:13;
   40:25)
3. What does God's holiness reveal about his love for his
   people? (Deut 7:6; Eph 5:25–27; Col 1:22; Heb 13:12;
   1 Pet 2:9)
4. How does the fact that God is holy encourage us to be
   prepared to trust him? (Isa 41:14; 43:15; 48:17)
5. What lessons for our lifestyle can we learn from the fact
   that God is holy? (Deut 23:14; Rom 12:1; 1 Cor 1:2; Eph 1:4;
   5:3; 1 Thess 3:13; 4:4,7)

Questions to think about

1. Is it possible to feel spiritually clean in the presence of
   God?
2. Why did a holy God choose to save unholy humanity?
3. What difference should the fact that God is holy have on
   our lifestyles?
4. What targets can we set to reflect God's character in us?

9 He's in charge and we're safe

Have you ever wondered:

- whether God actually knows what I am doing now?
- whether accidents occur without God's permission?
- why bad things happen to good people?
- whether God is with me in my darkness?

A few years ago we had a family holiday in Orlando, Florida, where the Disney parks and an assortment of water parks are located. The latter are vast areas of entertainment, all involving water. One of the experiences on offer was a tall water slide with a 30-metre vertical drop, the base of which curves into a shallow receiving pool. My young son was intrigued, and I rashly volunteered to join him. It involved a steep climb up steps to a platform where a number of lifeguards supervised two queues of mainly young people and directed them towards two gates. At this point, though my brain shouted, 'Go back', my embarrassment at the thought of going down the steps between the ascending crowds of ardent devotees overcame my common sense. Those about to undertake 'the experience of their lives' sat in front of the gates, crossed their arms over their chests and crossed their ankles. At a word from the lifeguard, each person shuffled to the edge of the slide, their legs dangling over the vertical drop. At that point, it was too late to go back. I was no longer in control of my destiny; the people waiting behind me were! With my son on the adjacent slide, I had no option but to launch off into the unknown. With my life flashing before my eyes and my heart beating far too quickly for my age, off I went.

Being out of control makes us vulnerable. It can fill us with fear, panic and a sense of isolation. Not being in control is an unpleasant experience. Yet it happens to us all the time. Circumstances change; life throws something unexpected at us. It's scary because not only do we feel *we're* not in control of our lives, but sometimes it feels as if no one else is either. Sometimes it seems that not even God is. But he *is* in control.

Through the years I have affirmed two maxims that are based on the evidence of the Bible. They are:

• an increasing readiness to relax because God's *in charge*
• an increasing readiness to relax because *God's* in charge

Moses was safe because God was in charge

Let me take you back a few thousand years to consider a man who knew what it was like to feel vulnerable. God had asked Moses to fulfil a mission that would create many enemies. He was asked to confront the most powerful man in the world, who was also the head of the most powerful religion in the world, and to do it as the representative of a God he had never seen. In order to support Moses, God convinced him that he was more in control of the situation than Moses could ever imagine. God showed Moses that he was on his side by working miracles that demonstrated that Moses was not on his own. A superior force was with him and was acting as his support.

At the same time, God demonstrated that he was against anyone or anything that may have sought to impede Moses. Every miracle that filled Moses with hope struck fear into the demonic forces who were against Moses. God was holding Moses tight; tighter than Moses realised.

The plagues God sent on the Egyptians achieved two objectives. First, they demonstrated to Moses (and to Pharaoh) that God intended to fulfil his desires. Moses was secure despite his apparent weakness compared to Pharaoh with his armies and gods. Secondly, they opposed the various deities of Egypt. Many Egyptian gods and goddesses were believed to have earthly representatives who received worship on their behalf. A number of the plagues undermined this worship by being directed to those representatives (Exod 12:12; 18:11).

For instance, when God turned the Nile into blood it was not just his way of supporting Moses' claims in Pharaoh's eyes; it was also a statement against the god of the Nile. The Egyptians believed that the god infused the river. Pharaoh's daughter bathed in it, not because it was the cleanest water but because she believed that the deity of the river would permeate her being as she did so. Along the river were over a hundred shrines, and the city of Nilopolis was a major centre for the worship of the river god. By turning the water into blood, God transformed something that represented life and fertility so that it represented death and sterility.

Similarly, frogs were believed to be the earthly representatives of fertility gods. God made a mockery of these so-called gods by increasing the animals' birth rate to such an unprecedented degree that the people had to kill them and burn them. God belittled the god that apparently owned the power of birth by arranging a population explosion of ridiculous proportions.

The plague of lice was particularly disruptive to the worship of the pagan gods because they rendered the priests ceremonially unclean, so that they could not serve in the temples. Thus the gods received no service or worship.

The darkness God sent was frightening and interrupted normal life, and it too was another statement against the demonic forces that took advantage of the peoples' superstitious beliefs. The Egyptians believed that the most powerful god was the Sun god, Ra. All the other temples faced east, where the Sun rose, as it was assumed to be the most superior god. But this symbol of life and light God cast into shade for three days.

The message of these and the other plagues is clear. When God commissions someone to act on his behalf, he arranges protection and support against all who may seek to put a stop to that activity. God provided protection for Moses and put his enemies in their place. Knowing that God is determined to do the same for all believers helps us to put our own lives into perspective.

Paul was safe because God was in charge

Thousands of years later, God arranged for another of his messengers to stand before another ruler, the head of the most powerful empire in the world at that time, who lived in a city dominated by the worship of many gods including himself. Like Moses, the apostle Paul was to enter a hostile environment with a message of freedom for people in bondage, though there was little reason to believe that many people would accept it.

Since Paul was delegated by God to undertake this mission, it was to be expected that evil forces would seek to undermine his plans. However, the final two chapters of Acts record that, despite all the events that could have terminated the mission, Paul arrived safely at his destination and, for two years, engaged in the work that God had called him to do (Acts 28:17–28). The reason for this is clear. God was in charge of the mission. Luke does not record whether Paul met the emperor, whether he established churches in Rome, what happened to him during those two years, whether he returned to Antioch or whether he died in Rome. What Luke does record in great detail is the sea voyage from Israel to Rome. He does so for a singular purpose: to demonstrate that God, who directs the destinies of his people, is sovereign. He ensures that he achieves his will through them despite the obstacles in the way.

So Luke records at length the problems the travellers encountered (Acts 27:7 – 28:6): the wind that made it difficult to sail and slowed them down, the indecision and unwise action of the captain, the fierce storm and darkness, the danger of starvation, the attempt by some of the crew to abandon the ship, the shipwreck, the soldiers' plan to kill the prisoners to forestall their escape, and Paul's snakebite. None of these obstacles was sufficient to disrupt God's plans for Paul. Why? Paul stated that *God* had determined that he would stand before Caesar (Acts 23:11; 27:24). Therefore, Paul could encourage everyone else not to fear, because his God could be trusted

This story is particularly significant in the first-century context. We must not forget the danger the Mediterranean Sea meant to the ancients. Today's cruise liners and ferries, which sail with accurate maritime aids, are very different from the primitive boats which faced the dangerous conditions during the first century.

Two of the main books used in the schools of the era were the *Odyssey* (traditionally viewed as the work of Homer) and Virgil's *Aeneid*. Each was used as a textbook that pupils read, memorised and dramatised. In particular, these books identified principles of life and conduct that helped to teach children how to become model citizens. They told of heroes who battled against the odds to cross the Greek (Mediterranean) Sea, overcoming the strategies of gods, storms and natural enemies along the way, until they achieved their objective. In the *Aeneid*, the prize is viewed as Rome, where Aeneas and his Trojan companions settled. The supremacy of the gods supporting these heroes is proved by their ability to support their protégés against all the obstacles that faced them.

Luke wrote the book of Acts for mainly Gentile readers. They were familiar with such epics and the messages they presented. In his account of Paul's sea voyage, Luke demonstrates that the God who protects Paul is superior to all other gods because he shields him as he crosses the hazardous Greek Sea from Israel to Rome. His Christian readers can take heart that the God who protected Paul is committed to protecting them too. At the same time, those who don't trust God are encouraged to transfer their allegiance to the one whose authority is supreme. The last verse of the book of Acts emphasises this unprecedented authority: Paul is recorded as preaching the kingdom of God and teaching about the Lord Jesus Christ 'boldly and without hindrance'. The final word in the original Greek means 'unhindered'. Luke's last word on the life of Paul reminds the readers that God, who reigns in supreme power, was supervising Paul's destiny and nothing could obstruct him.

God overshadowed Paul, guiding him and controlling his destiny in even the most hostile circumstances. The same God controls the lives of every other believer. We may not always feel that we have a hold on God, but he always has a hold on us. Christ has ascended, but he is not absent.

When things go wrong, God is still in charge

When things go wrong, it isn't necessarily because we have sinned or stepped out of God's will or because the devil caused it. Often it occurs because we are part of a world that has not been right since sin slid into the Garden of Eden. Whatever the cause of our problems, God is not absent from us. The most evil act in history was the crucifixion of Jesus. There it appeared that God was not in control, but that wicked people, operating their own selfish agenda, were directing the destiny of Jesus. In reality, God was still in control, as Peter affirmed in his speech on the Day of Pentecost: '[Jesus] was handed over to you by God's set purpose and foreknowledge' (Acts 2:23).

We don't have the answers to many of life's problems and traumas. But what we do have is the certainty that God is still in charge. Safety and security are found not in the absence of danger but in the presence of God. The earliest days of the church saw a devastating catalogue of natural calamities including famines, earthquakes and plagues, as well as verbal and physical attacks on Christians, resulting in countless martyrdoms. Christians were not safeguarded from the events of that era. What they had to learn was that these events did not separate them from God. Most people of the time thought the gods were not interested in their situations, much less that they could be bothered to get involved in their lives. The message of the Bible is that God is so interested that he came into this world in the person of Jesus to show how much he wanted to infuse us with his presence and resources. His purpose is to make a difference in our lives and in the situations in which we find ourselves.

God holds our destiny in his hands, whatever it might be, whether life or death, a pension or martyrdom. He is in control and never out of control. There's never a panic in heaven. God is in control even when it feels as if no one is in control. He is looking after us even when it feels that no one is looking after us. He is determined to give us whatever is best for us and to fulfil his will in our lives. Because he has supreme authority he can do whatever he wants. The psalmist declares, 'The LORD does whatever pleases him, in the heavens and on the earth' (135:6). Paul affirms that God will ensure that the work he has started in our lives is completed (Phil 1:6), while Peter confirms that we are 'shielded by God's power' (1 Pet 1:5).

It is no surprise that many of God's names relate to his sovereignty. The first book of the Bible emphasises that he is God Most High (Gen 14:20), God Almighty (17:1) and Sovereign Lord (15:2). The final book of the Bible gives God similar titles, including Lord God Almighty (Rev 1:8) and God the Almighty (19:16), while the final chapter refers to God's throne (22:1). It is as if the writers want the readers to be assured from first to last that, whatever life and the future hold, God controls both, and it's easy for him. The more we fill our minds with these certain truths, the more our lives will radiate peace and security.

When he speaks, the earth shakes.
When he walks, creation watches.
When he looks, silence reigns.
Where he treads, he claims.

Where he lives, he reigns,
for he is King.

He has no foes who trouble him;
no enemy who causes stress or strain;
no force that makes him catch his breath
or struggle, slow down,
or even think of moving back again.

Like a noble lion, he moves, in serene
and awesome majesty
and wherever we, his cubs, are,
the Lion King is near.

He is our shade and strength,
our stream in the desert,
our nest in the thorn bush,
our pocket in the crush of life.

We are safe because we are in his palm
as is the world in which we are.
He breathes calm into our lives
and folds us into his love.
He whispers peace
and ripples stillness
into our storms
for he is in charge
of all we are.

Questions for discussion

1. What evidence is there that God supervises our lives?
   (1 Pet 5:1)

2. How should we think when life seems unfair? (Isa 45:17;
   Eph 1:11; James 1:2–4)

3. How does Psalm 23 show how God watches over and cares for us?

4. In what ways did God supervise Jesus in his life and ministry?

5. How does God's peace link with his authority? (Eph 2:14,15; Phil 4:9; 1 Thess 5:23)

Questions to think about

1. What difference does the fact that God is sovereign make to the way you face the future?

2. Why doesn't God demonstrate his sovereignty clearly in the world today?

3. How would you counsel a believer who is struggling to find God in his or her suffering?

4. Since he has the power to end all suffering, why doesn't he do so?

10 He knows all and we can trust him

Have you ever wondered:

- whether God knows the future?
- how involved God is in my destiny?
- whether God knows what will happen to me tomorrow?
- whether our prayers can affect the future if God already knows it?

The thing we can be most certain of is the past – it has happened and, though we might wish to change some of it, we can't. The thing we can be least certain about is what hasn't happened yet – the future. The future is an object of speculation. Are we going to pass or fail that exam, have two children or none, be in the same job in three years' time or not, be alive in five years' time or not? The future is exciting just because it is uncertain; changes that may be very positive can occur. However, it's also a little scary because the events it brings may turn hope to hopelessness. Would I choose to know the future if it was possible so to do? The fact is, I don't know what tomorrow holds, but God does.

God knows everything

It stretches my imagination to breaking-point when I try to understand that God knows everything. God doesn't need to learn; he has no need to engage in study or research, because he knows more than any number of encyclopedias can hold. Not only does he know every fact there is to know, but he also understands everything. He knows when a leaf falls in a forest, where it falls and why it falls. He knows how many stars exist and why; he even knows their names (Ps 147:4). I know that the clouds hang in the sky; God knows how they do so (Job 37:16). He knows that we are individually distinct from other people but he also knows why we are all different. Job declared that God 'sees everything under the heavens' (Job 28:24), while Psalm 147:5 states that 'his understanding has no limit'.

The fact that God knows everything brings many benefits to us as Christians:

First, we needn't fear that God loves us only because he can't see the sinful parts of our lives. He knows everything about us, the good, the bad and the ugly, and still remains committed to us. David came to the same conclusion when he acknowledged, 'Lord, you have searched me and you know me', and said such knowledge was too wonderful for him (Ps 139:1,6). Far from causing him embarrassment or fear, it delighted him because it combated his anxieties while at the same time enabling him to benefit from the Lord's knowledge of his progress (Ps 139:23,24).

This characteristic of God is very important, for it means we can accept that God loves us unconditionally. This is the greatest form of love; everyone wants to know they are loved no matter what. This is never completely possible between humans because no one can know someone else perfectly. But God does, and he loves us eternally despite what he knows about us. There is nothing in us that God doesn't already know. He's never surprised by our actions or thoughts. This doesn't mean he is indifferent to our sins, but it does mean that he is never going to come across something in us that takes him by surprise and stops him loving us.

Secondly, because he knows all our circumstances we are secure whatever they are. He does not function like the emergency services, who answer our call and have to find out where we are and what we need. He hears us before we breathe the words; they are recorded by him before we rehearse them in our minds. Jesus encourages his disciples by reminding them that 'even the very hairs of your head are all numbered' (Matt 10:30). He always knows what's around the corner. He reigns in calm tranquillity.

Thirdly, given that he knows everything, he can't possibly make a mistake. He cannot initiate any flawed activity. Error is not possible with God.

Fourthly, we don't need to remind him about anything. God does not need a shopping-list, memos or a diary. The angels are not his secretaries, reminding God of his appointments and daily agenda. Instead, they ensure that his sovereign, wise plans are carried out. We could never inform God of something he did not already know about. He knows all there is to know, now and for ever.

Finally, he is unique and we worship him as the Incomparable One (Isa 55:9).

God knows more than we do

Of course, saying that God knows more than we do is to state the obvious, but still it's helpful to do so. Change occurs so rapidly today that knowledge quickly gets outdated in all disciplines. I heard of a scientist who was asked how many subatomic particles had been discovered. Looking at his watch, he said, 'At this moment in time, the number of subatomic particles that have been discovered is ...' and then named a figure in the hundreds. He knew that technological advances were so rapid that the number could change very quickly. It helps us to be humble when we recognise that the more we know, the more we realise there is to know. The quest for knowledge can be fulfilling but also frustrating. However much the whole of humanity put together may know, there are enormous gaps in our knowledge. We only have to think of the enormity of space, the complexity of the human body or the mystery of life itself to know how true this is.

Job was drawn into a one-sided conversation with God in which God told him that many aspects of life were outside Job's knowledge (38:1–41). 'Where were you when I laid the earth's foundation?' he asked. 'Have you journeyed to the springs of the sea or walked in the recesses of the deep?' 'Do you know the laws of the heavens?' 'Who has the wisdom to count the clouds?'(vs 4,16,33,37).

God was seeking not to humiliate Job, but to remind him that his knowledge was limited. This fact helped Job by putting into perspective his own questions about his suffering. He did not understand or know why it was happening, but God revealed that *he* did. The one who gives orders to the morning, who knows how to limit the power of the sea and who fathers the rain would not allow Job to fall from his grip. Job concludes, 'My ears had heard of you but now my eyes have seen you' (42:5). When we catch a glimpse into the mind of God we wonder why we ever worried.

When our son Luke was a toddler and before he could talk, he taught us an important lesson. As we came home late one evening, he tried to get our attention by pointing to the dark skies. We couldn't determine what it was that had struck him so forcibly, but his excitement was contagious. Eventually, we realised it was the moon. Something we were used to was a miracle to him when he saw it for the first time. Since then, I have made it my aim to never lose the sense of wonder that comes from considering God's creation; a complex tapestry of unimaginable and breathtaking beauty in all its manifestations, making us gasp in admiration and awe at the excellence of such a wise God.

God knows everything about the future

The Bible is clear that God knows the future. Isaiah 42:9 tells us that God declares the future before it happens. Jesus knew that Judas would betray him and that Peter would deny him. God's complete knowledge of the future can be profoundly encouraging because it indicates that everything is under his control, even the things and situations that don't exist yet.

But the fact that God knows the future also raises serious questions. For example, if God knows the future, what's the point of praying? How can God know about things that haven't happened yet? Doesn't it mean that God predetermines the future and that therefore people have no free will?

First, although our explanations may be limited or even non-existent, we must let the Bible state the facts about God, however incompatible with our understanding they may be. Since God is incomparable, we do well to reflect on the words of Paul:

> 'Oh, the depth of the riches of the wisdom and knowledge
> of God!
> How unsearchable his judgments,
> and his paths beyond tracing out!
> "Who has known the mind of the Lord?
> Or who has been his counsellor?"'

(Rom 11:33,34)

Although it is valuable to explore God, there comes a time when we have to acknowledge that 'mystery' is the best word to describe him. To admit that God is mysterious and therefore fundamentally unknowable in his entirety is to accept what the Bible says even when it does not fit with our wisdom.

Secondly, some have suggested that God is outside time; he knows what will occur in future time but does not determine the way people act. He knows what will occur without determining that it will occur., God knows what I will do next, but the fact that he knows this doesn't mean I am forced to do it. Indeed, if I did something different, that wouldn't make God wrong, because he would know that I was going to do something different. Perhaps God knows the future only partially? But that would place him at the mercy of the future, significantly undermining the security of Christians and making a nonsense of Paul's encouraging words to the church in Philippi: 'he who began a good work in you will carry it on to completion' (Phil 1:6).

Thirdly, the fact that God knows the future does not release individuals from taking responsibility for their actions. The Bible holds both these factors in tension and does not seek to resolve or explain the apparent paradox. Proverbs 16:9 states: 'In his heart a man plans his course, but the Lord determines his steps.' The Bible does not permit us to have a fatalistic approach to life, viewing God as making the future happen in a particular way, so that people feel powerless. Both God and individuals are responsible for the future. There is a mystery here, but it is better to acknowledge that mystery and live with the Bible's tension than to try to unravel it in a way that the Bible chooses not to do.

Similarly, the interaction between prayer and the will of God is a mystery, in part. On the one hand, it is very simple. Prayer is communication with God, but it is also God's way of communicating with us. It is not the only means; he speaks to us in the Bible and through the Spirit. But God can also make his will known to us in prayer. Prayer is not an opportunity for us to get God to change his mind or get him to do want we want, but an opportunity for God to help us pray as he would pray if he were praying with us. Prayer is valuable, not as a means of changing the future, but as a way to engage with God in bringing the future into reality in the present.

God is wise in the use of his knowledge

Not only does God know everything but, more importantly, he uses his knowledge carefully and wisely. The Bible's God is not a detached superbrain. Rather, he uses his knowledge for the benefit of his creation. The Bible often links God's knowledge with his wisdom (eg Rom 11:33). At the same time, wisdom is often associated with God's power. God knows the best course of action and has the power to take it. His wisdom may sometimes be recognised as such only when looking back and, in some cases, that will mean when we reach the other side of death. It was years after his brothers had sold him into slavery that Joseph was able to acknowledge that 'it was not you who sent me here, but God' (Gen 45:8).

God does what pleases him

Allied closely to his wisdom and power is the fact that God does only what pleases him (Isa 46:10). This flows logically from the fact that he knows everything and uses his knowledge wisely. But now it includes a personal dimension, that of pleasure. God is pleased to act in the way he does. The implications for believers are significant. God knows all about us (Ps 139:2-4). He chooses to develop our lives wisely (Eph 1:11) on the basis of his incomparable authority (Dan 4:35), but also is motivated to bring it to fruition because he is pleased to do so. Psalm 115:3 states that 'he does whatever pleases him'. These truths draw us to worship, as we recognise that the one who knows us intimately chooses to safeguard us for the eternal future that he has planned with us in mind.

> *I watched it uncertain, afraid to let go.*
> *It struggled to hold on, fluttering to and fro.*
> *The leaf held on with all its might.*
> *To the tree it held tight*
> *and all the while the wind softly caressed it and*
> *encouraged it to fly*
> *But it resisted the pull.*
> *It was safe where it was.*
> *Who knew where the wind would blow?*

And all the while, the wind warmly caressed it and
encouraged it to fly.

One day it did. Tired of holding on, it let go
and prepared to flutter down
to the dirt below where it knew it would die.
But the wind that had gently plucked it from the tree
tucked it under its arm
and took it high, far higher than ever it had dreamed it
could go.
Once it was tied to the tree
but now it was free on the breeze.

Lord, I wish I was that leaf. I wish I could trust you so
completely, to know you hold me, and sense your peace.
But, I'm afraid Lord, afraid to let go. I fear the future;
where might I go? What if I fail? What will letting go entail,
Lord?

'Son, trust in my Spirit, the Breeze.
His love for you is what sets you free.
He says that he'll change you, but love is his mould.
He promises to hold you, but tight in his fold.
He promises to use you, but it's all in his love.
You'll fly – but remember your teacher's a dove.
And together you'll fly in peace on the breeze.
His love for you is what gives you peace.
For my will for you is not a sigh or a rod;
it's a song, to take you high, to me, your God.
My Spirit in you is all you need
to be assured that I love you;
for you belong to me.'

Questions for discussion

1. What difference does the fact that God has perfect knowledge make to our present circumstances? (Ps 103:14; 139:2–4; John 10:14)

2. What difference does knowing that God has perfect knowledge make to your thoughts about the future? (Job 23:10; Dan 2:22; Isa 55:9)

3. How can we receive some of God's wisdom? (Ps 111:10; 119:99; Col 3:16)

4. What most impresses you about God's knowledge? (Ps 147:5; Isa 65:24; Acts 15:18)

Questions to think about

1. Does God determine our future or do we have a measure of free will?

2. If God knows the future, why should we pray about events to come?

3. Since God knows all about us, why does he still love us?

4. Does the fact that God knows everything concern, impress or please you? Why?

11 He never leaves us

Have you ever wondered:

- what it was like for Jesus to have been forsaken by his Father when dying on the cross?
- what it would be like to lose your family and friends?
- what it means when Jesus says he'll never leave us?
- where God is and how close he is to us?

It was 27 May, ten minutes to midnight. I was in a hospital corridor and Judy was in an adjoining ward. I was on the phone to my mother. My initial words to her were, 'It's a boy!' Our first child, Luke, was born. He had big brown eyes and soft blond curls. He grew to be a quiet, attentive child who never found it hard to say sorry; the kind of boy teachers loved to have in their classes. But along with this sensitivity went a gentleness and vulnerability. How would he cope with his first day in nursery, in school? Would he be able to handle disappointment, bullies, exams or all the other hurdles children have to overcome? Would he get through adolescence unscathed, or would he be marred for life? His early years were times of reflection (no different from those of many other parents) when we learned to recognise that Luke was not going anywhere on his own. Someone who loved him far more than even we could goes with him wherever he goes; God is with him. A few days after he went to university, he sent us the poem that concludes Chapter 3, in which he sought to describe something of his awareness and appreciation of God.

While we were wondering whether he would cope, we were learning that God was making sure he would. Since then, he has been on missions to the foothills of the Himalayas, the vast spaces of Kenya and the beautiful mountains of South Africa. All the time, we have been learning to recognise that Luke has never been on his own.

God has chosen never to leave us

To discover the incredible nature of the truth that God is always with us, we have to travel back in time to that moment when Jesus walked directly into sin's most concentrated radiation and allowed himself to be touched by its curse. By that act of self-sacrifice, he broke the chain reaction that was sending us headlong into an eternity away from God. He broke the power of sin over our lives. We came through into life because he went through into death. He who is unapproachable in majesty, in need of nothing and no one, uniquely self-sufficient and absolutely complete, dedicated himself to die for people who couldn't find him and who weren't even looking. The Christians in Rome, who knew what it was like to be alienated and made to feel unwanted, and who experienced the ferocity of the first persecutions, were reminded by Paul that it was impossible for them to be separated from God (Rom 8:38,39).

He who has already achieved so much for us will not give up on us now. Instead, he gives us the Spirit to stay with us to the end (Phil 1:6). He is in our lives not simply to keep us on the straight and narrow; not to act as a heavenly bouncer to keep us in line. He is not a policeman from paradise, a matron with attitude, a headmaster with a stick, a chain around our legs or a straitjacket to keep us holy. Rather, he is our bodyguard, our tour guide to get us to our destination and to make sure that we enjoy the journey. His role is not just to be there when we need him but to be there when we don't. He keeps us safe so that we shall receive our inheritance, a life with God for ever (Eph 1:14). But also he keeps us because we are God's inheritance (Eph 1:18).

God holds you tighter than you know

Some years ago, we went on holiday as a family to the Mediterranean. It was Luke who, as a young teenager, decided that we should have a go at paragliding. I wasn't so sure, but when he expressed such enthusiasm and so enjoyed the experience, I thought maybe I should follow his example. Judy had a go, so how could I not?

It was my first and last paragliding experience. Having given my life savings for 15 minutes of terror in the skies, I was harnessed to the gear by two bronzed young men who made my untanned body look unprepared for such a close brush with the sun.

A coil of rope joined me to a speedboat that was rapidly shrinking as it sped into the distance. At the same time, I stood on the deck and watched it become clouded by the spray that was churned up by its powerful double engines, while the coil of rope before my feet unravelled all too quickly. There was no turning back. Soon I would move to the end of the deck and be catapulted into space. Before I had time to cultivate a nonchalant air, I shot into the sky and into the future. Before I knew it, I was above the hotels, above the birds, above the world.

But I had a problem. I couldn't enjoy the experience because I couldn't remember whether I was to hold on to the harness or whether I could relax my grip. My brain said that I wasn't expected to hold on tightly to stop slipping through the harness but my heart wasn't so sure. So I held on. By the time I arrived back on solid ground, my fingers had to be prised from the harness, they had become welded to the rope. I had not needed to hang on so tightly. I could have relaxed, because the harness was holding me tight.

It is liberating to recognise that God is a secure harness who wraps himself around our lives and never lets us go. Of course, this does not mean that we are protected from problems and pain, but it does mean that we never go through them alone.

Empty promises

We live in a world that has grown accustomed to words that have no substance and tired of them, from the casual 'I'll phone you later' to government promises of millions of dollars for international aid. We have become sceptical if not cynical, because words such as 'trust' and 'faithfulness' are used with less and less integrity. The junk mail promises us a prize if only we ring a number or listen to a presentation or send for some information, but we know that if it sounds too good to be true it probably is. God is very different. His promises *do* sound too good to be true, and yet they *are* true. God has always been the exception. By definition, he is faithful and trustworthy (Deut 7:9).

Eternal promises

Over two thousand years ago a group of Christians, who had experienced only peace, joy and hope in their new faith, were beginning to struggle with emotions they had never faced before. They felt fear, anxiety and regret. A fog of fear was drifting into their days; they were strangers in their own streets, and it felt lonely. It was made worse by the fact that only a few years earlier Jesus had said he was coming back again, and they were still waiting. Now their friends were being arrested, imprisoned and rejected, and they were feeling abandoned, deserted and lost.

The book of Hebrews was written to these people, and the writer had a single message to encourage and stabilise them: Jesus was superior to anyone they can imagine, and God was always with them (Heb 13:5). God's promise, 'I will never leave you; never will I forsake you', is a quote from Deuteronomy 31:6. There, God made this promise to Moses and the Israelites before the people crossed the River Jordan and entered the land that God had promised them when he rescued them from slavery in Egypt. Moses, who had led them thus far, was not going to lead them into Israel. The people were inevitably concerned, since many battles lay ahead and they were going without Moses.

Joshua was to become their leader, but he was inexperienced and knew it. If *they* felt uncertain, how lonely did *he* feel? Maybe that's why God echoed the same promise to him (Deut 31:8). God gave them all the same message: 'I'm going with you.'

God makes the same promise to Christians today. He doesn't change, and neither do his promises.

The promise in Hebrews 13:5, 'God has said, "Never will I leave you; never will I forsake you"', is even more emphatic in its original language, Greek.

- It emphasises just who is making the promise: 'for he himself has said …'
- The first part of the promise could be translated, 'I will never, never leave you.' It's not just that God promises never to leave us; he promises never to be unable to help us when we need him; He's failure proof.
- The final part of the promise could be translated, 'I will never, never, never forsake you.'
- The promise is made to each Christian individually rather than to the church as a whole; the word 'you' is singular, not plural. This is God's personal commitment to each of his people.

Guaranteed promises

For years I have noted all my appointments and lists of things to do in a diary. It is central to my working day, but I still forget to fulfil some functions. Either I forget to record something or I miss it on the page. Sometimes it means I break a promise. I haven't intended to break it; it's not that I didn't want to keep it; it's often just simple forgetfulness. But God *can't* break his promises. He is trustworthy, and his promises can bear all the weight we place on them.

A pastor visited a Christian in his nineties and found him very troubled. The problem soon tumbled out: the old man had been losing his memory. What distressed him most was that he couldn't remember the many Bible verses he had learnt over the years. The pastor's response was timely 'You may have forgotten God's promises, but God hasn't.'

Powerful personal promises

I was brought up to believe that my salvation and my growth as a Christian depended on me. 'Take one step to God and then he'll take two steps to you,' I was told. It took me many years to realise that God was more interested in my spiritual development than I was, and that he had given me the resources and constant support of the ever-present Spirit to enable me to grow.

For much of my life I was like a man shovelling coal into the boiler to provide the energy to keep the train going. He has no time to enjoy the journey; he's too busy ensuring that he gets to the end of the line. I am learning to recognise that power source is not my effort alone but external, like the trains that run on electricity. They don't need fuel; they need brakes. The electricity is pulsating, the energy is ready to be unleashed, the train is resourced from an energy base outside itself. That's what gets the train to the destination.

Charlton Heston was once practising for the chariot race in the epic film *Ben Hur*. He told the director, Cecil B de Mille, 'I'll never win the race. I can hardly stay on the chariot.' The great director said, 'You just get on the chariot and hang on; it's my job to make sure you win.' Our role is to start the journey; it's God's role to make sure we reach the destination.

When we recognise God's inexplicable commitment to us we surely feel deep gratitude. Rather than taking God for granted because he's always there, we are led to a deep sense of awe. God is awesome.

While the eagle's chicks squawked in the nest on the cliff
the eagle would soar on the breeze and drift
and when the time came for the chicks to fly
despite their anxious fluttering cries

*they had nothing to fear
for the wings of the eagle were near.*

*In the storm that smashed into Galilee
were a frightened group of men.
They were powerless and helpless to fend
off the wind
but Jesus was with them right then.*

*When those fearful disciples heard Jesus say
'I want you to go; make disciples today',
their hearts began beating,
for each of them knew
they could not achieve it
unless he was there too.*

*The question for them and the one that we feel
is 'How do I know if he'll be there for me,
my companion, my song, my close harmony?'
For if it's really true that he'll be
my songmaker, my melody,
then no one and nothing can obstruct
his working out his will in me.*

*For you the past has gone
but some of it is stained
with memories you wish weren't there.
Don't let them restrict you or cause you fear
for the one who knows you always stands near,
not in the shadows on the edge of your life,
but as central to you as is husband to wife.*

*The God who made you,
put colour in your hair,
is the one who lovingly says,
'For ever, I care.'*

Questions for discussion

1. How can we know that God can be trusted? (Deut 7:9;
   Ps 36:5; 89:8; Lam 3:22,23)

2. How does God show himself faithful in his relationship
   with us? (Ps 119:75; 145:3; 1 Cor 1:9; 10:13; 1 Thess 5:24)

3. How can the fact that God can be trusted make a difference
   to our concept of the future? (Ps 31:23; Phil 1:6; 2 Tim 1:12;
   1 Pet 4:19)

4. How does it change our lives when we grasp the truth that
   God is faithful to us? (2 Tim 2:13; 1 John 1:9)

Questions to think about

1. What impact does the fact that God is faithful have on our
   lives and futures?

2. In what ways can we reflect God's faithfulness in our
   behaviour?

3. What is God's greatest expression of faithfulness to you?

4. How can we increasingly appreciate God's faithfulness?

12 He's always saying 'Hello'

Have you ever wondered:

- how God is involved in prayer?
- whether prayer is one-way or two-way communication?
- whether God's role is to listen while I talk, or whether I am supposed to listen as well?
- how to listen to God?

I hate sermons on prayer. They fill me with guilt and drive me to despair. The preacher describes prayer as able to move mountains; as interaction with the Almighty; as the springboard to a God-anointed life. He reminds me that revivals are born in prayer.

I say 'Amen' to it all, but inwardly I cringe. Satan creeps on to my shoulder and whispers 'Fraud!', while my conscience reminds me that as a prayer warrior I'm a failure. My most common prayers are fairly short: 'Thank you' and 'Sorry'.

If the preacher asks me if I want to develop a better prayer life, or even a prayer life that has some hope of improvement, he can't lose. With prayer, I'm at my weakest. What does he want me to do? Come to the front, receive prayer, stand on my head? I'll do it, if only I can clamber over this prayer mountain, this hurdle that's too high – just so that next time he preaches on prayer I can look him in the eye and say, 'It's OK now. I've got this prayer problem under control.' If only!

My experiences so far have not always helped me. Three issues used to dominate my prayer life in my early years as a Christian – methods, the Bible and guilt. The Quiet Time was a part of my daily life – a time of reading the Bible and prayer. It was foundational to my development, but rarely an easy task. And that was the problem: it was a task, a discipline. In fact, when I thought of prayer, I quickly associated it with the word 'discipline'. Prayer was something one had to do; a discipline to be learnt; a practice to be worked at. Strangely enough, words like 'liberty', 'joy' or 'Wow!' did not come to my mind when I thought of prayer. I learnt how to engage in 'Seven Minutes with God' and other methods developed to help people like me through the tiresome battlefield of prayer. Don't misunderstand me – prayer wasn't always hard work, and neither is discipline (a word that should not be far from a disciple who is developing in prayer). The problem for me was that it was the *only* word I associated with prayer.

Prayer that didn't have a significant element of sacrifice about it was somehow questionable, deficient, if not counterfeit. Prayer that took place in the early hours when all my friends were asleep was worth more than the prayer offered during the lunch break. During my youth, a famous evangelist came to my city. He prayed at 6 am and he was a successful evangelist. His early prayer time was surely an important key to his effectiveness. Sure enough, even though he did not encourage anyone to follow his pattern for prayer, I got up at 6 am to pray. But I fell asleep somewhere in the middle of the prayer. The next morning I was determined to do better, but I didn't. The following morning I gave up. Maybe I should have persevered. There was another of my keywords when it came to prayer: perseverance. People who pray must be passionate and persevering, and too often I lacked both characteristics. I lived with the guilt of those failures for many years. Only later in my Christian journey did I realise that prayer is very personal, and that many of the burdens we carry concerning it are self-imposed.

We are often misled into trying to follow the agendas and guidelines that God has given to others, without first checking whether they are appropriate for us. If they are, we can learn from the experiences of those who are following a similar pattern. If they are not, we should discover the prayer pilgrimage that is appropriate for us and follow it faithfully, learning to develop it along the way. For some Christians, the morning is the best time to be with God; for others, the best time may be last thing at night. Others try to build time with God into the course of their day. Prayer is not a competition; it's a conversation, a way of life. That means it's very personal to each Christian.

Something else that increased my frustration with myself was what I read in the Bible. It shone its spotlight on me and what it showed up wasn't pleasant. Jesus spent whole nights in prayer! Now, I've done that in my time. I was a missionary for a year. Every Friday my team spent the night in prayer. But somehow Friday nights didn't seem to match up to the nights Jesus spent in prayer. Paul didn't help either; he told the Thessalonian Christians to pray continually (1 Thess 5:17), and they'd only been Christians for a few months! Paul was expecting them to do what I could only dream about – though it was more of a nightmare than a dream! What did Paul mean, anyway? How can anyone pray continually?

All this deepened my reservoir of guilt while my surface Christian face betrayed none of it. How could I share such failings with other Christians, who seemed not to experience my battles with prayer? Older Christians sometimes plunged me under the waters of guilt until I nearly drowned with such encouragements as these:

'If the Queen was here, your mind wouldn't wander!'

'Jesus died on the cross for you and you can't even stay awake for a few minutes to pray!'

'What do you think you're going to do in heaven if you don't pray now?'

The thought of heaven as one eternal prayer meeting didn't help me, until I began to rethink prayer.

And so began my journey as a prayer pilgrim. This chapter

shares some of the lessons I'm learning along the way.

Prayer is primarily an encounter with God

For most of my life, I've identified prayer with talking to God. Of course, that's part of prayer, and I endorse the importance of prayer meetings and personal conversational prayer. But I'm learning that talking to God is only a part of prayer. I am learning to define prayer as a God-conscious event; it's a time when I'm conscious of God, when heaven breaks into my life on earth, when the transcendent God who created the universe opens a window in my world and says, 'Hello, Keith.' God's interruption establishes an encounter with him and, in that encounter, a prayer is born. No words need to be spoken; it's enough that I have become aware of God. I am learning to define those encounters as prayers. It's not the only form of prayer, but it's still prayer, initiated by God. The psalmist appears to be speaking of a similar experience when he encourages his readers to be quiet and, in that stillness, to acknowledge the presence of God. 'Hush – God's here' (see Ps 46:10).

Sometimes I work at home. Picture the scene. I'm engrossed in my studies, but later in the day a key turns in the lock of our front door. My wife Judy has come home. I've not seen her yet; no words have been spoken but a range of emotions, thoughts and feelings have been sparked off within me. At that moment, words are not as important as the fact that I am conscious of her presence. An encounter has already taken place in my mind. I'm learning to see prayer like this, as encounters with God when he opens a door into my life and, without words, I'm aware that he's there. One of the most sobering verses in the Bible is Genesis 28:16, in which Jacob says, 'Surely the LORD is in this place, and I was not aware of it.' We need to learn not to miss God when he visits us.

A poor man sat in church. He'd been there for hours, just sitting. The minister came up to him and asked if he was all right.

He said that he was, and explained what he had been doing. 'I've been looking at God, God's been looking at me, and we're happy together.' He had learnt to encounter God without spoiling that intimacy with speech.

Prayer doesn't have to be frenetic or hard work. Prayer is the excitement of encountering God, of experiencing a God-conscious moment. It may involve words; it may not. This is what I'm learning.

Prayer is learning to encounter God in his world

I am learning to listen for the key in the lock when God opens a door into my life and says, 'Hello, it's me again.' It happens more times than we realise. I remember seeing my daughter sitting in church with her friends. As I saw her, I had an encounter with God. Anna-Marie was laughing, full of life, fresh, pretty, vivacious – and then she saw me looking at her through the ranks of people in church, and she smiled. It was a father–daughter moment and I felt proud, but I also felt God. It was as if he said, 'I've made her the girl she is; the person she's going to be.' It was a God-conscious moment; when God said 'Hello' and, in effect, 'Relax, I'm in charge.'

I think of times when my students and I have explored the Bible. We have asked questions and even perhaps discovered answers. Sometimes, the answers surprise and stimulate us. In those times, we are encountering God. We often respond to those encounters with words that don't seem to belong to prayer, such as 'Wow!' or 'That's remarkable!' or 'Mmm – I've never thought of that before.' God has opened his Word and said 'Hello', and we've replied 'Wow!'

With colleagues and students, I have often explored aspects of God and his dealings with us. In our creative probing we have tried to tap into the inexhaustible nature of God. As we do, before we know it we find that, while we are encountering each other as Christians in our quest of God, we are encountering God himself. We haven't prayed, and yet we have, for we have encountered God. We haven't stopped to pray, but he has stepped in to say 'Hello'.

One of my students came to our college from Korea. Before her arrival she had suffered a major accident that caused a severe loss of memory. Nevertheless, throughout her time as a student she was conscientious and caring, faithful in the smallest details, which few others noticed. I noticed. She now serves the Lord in an isolated region of Northern Ghana. When I think of In-Hee, God speaks to me and says 'Hello'.

I am learning to recognise that prayer is to encounter God and to listen for his 'Hello' in people around me, in circumstances good and bad (2 Cor 1:9; 1 Thess 2:2), in his creation, in his Word, and even in me. This is probably the kind of prayer-consciousness Paul had in mind when he encouraged his readers to be faithful in prayer (Rom 12:12).

Prayer means responding to God as well as speaking to God

In his book *Working the Angles*, Eugene Peterson speaks of 'the overwhelming previousness of God's speech to our prayers'. Prayer is not always a matter of me saying 'Hello' to God; it's often God who's the first to say 'Hello'. Many of my prayers do consist of me saying 'Hello', and, of course, that's fine. But how many times does God start the conversation and we just don't hear him?

When my daughter was very young, I was driving to the airport with her to pick up Judy. 'Why doesn't God speak to me?' Anna-Marie asked. I knew what she meant. As Christians, we talk about God speaking to us but we have very limited notions as to how he does so. Perhaps he will speak through a sermon, a prophecy or our personal Bible-reading. Few of us expect an audible voice or an angelic visitation. But the fact is, he's everywhere, and I'm learning the importance of identifying where he is so that I can respond to him, whatever he says, however he says it. Paul anticipated this when he wrote to the church in the bustling metropolis of Rome and reminded the believers that God whispers his presence throughout his creation (Rom 1:20).

I remember reading a book that offered many guidelines for getting God's attention. But we don't need to learn how to get God's attention. He's already perfectly attentive to us. Instead, I am learning how to listen for him.

You may have heard the old story of a group of radio operators turning up for an interview and being shown into a crowded waiting-room to await their turn. The call never came. After some uncertainty, one man jumped out of his chair and ran into the interview room, emerging a few minutes later to announce that he had been offered the job – to the astonishment of those present. He told them to listen and, sure enough, a message was being tapped out in Morse code, informing them that the first person who responded to it and came into the interview room would be offered the job. But only one man was listening.

I've often assumed that God is to be encountered in the magnificent, the extraordinary, the sensational and the atmospherically charged (and sometimes he is). But I'm learning that he is also encountered in the ordinary events of life.

Prayer is very personal

God loves us individually and perfectly. He loves us uniquely and differently. He therefore encounters each of us differently. He says 'Hello' to each of us, countless times every day. But he does so in different ways, depending on who we are and how we are. That's the way a good father relates to his children, and God is the best father there is.

So rejoice in your individuality. Refuse to be driven to feel that you have to relate to God in any way other than that which he has chosen for you. Don't let God's agenda for others burden you. Be true to yourself as the person God is making you. Listen out for God, for he speaks to us in our own accents so that we can recognise him.

The Bible reflects a remarkable variety of forms of prayer, depending on who is praying and what the circumstances are (1 Kings 8:54; Ps 35:13; Matt 26:39). Some of us encounter God in loud worship, others in silence; some in the magnificent, others in the ordinary; some in written prayers, others with songs of praise, and yet others with tears. Be aware of who you are and listen for God to speak to you in ways that he knows are appropriate for you. Then be creative in your response to him.

Have you ever wondered whether we'll pray in heaven? We'll certainly encounter God there – in each other, in the angels, in our conversations, our excitement, our humour, our discussions, our plans, our memories and our dreams. Everything will reflect God. In heaven he will be reflected perfectly, but even in this dark world he's still God and it's still his world and he still sparkles in it. At times, his light rushes towards us like a searchlight; at other times, it's like a candle beckoning us softly to follow. In all these ways God is saying, 'Here I am; I've just called to say "Hello".' And when we say 'Hello' to God in response, a prayer is born as we encounter him in our lives.

I can't begin to imagine what God's got in store in heaven for me,
but it'll keep me content for eternity
for God will be in it, I'm sure.

I want to explore and gaze at the places I've never been to before.
I want to climb the mountains on the moon and paddle to the distant shore
of a desert island, and then explore some more,
and all I see will reflect God, I'm sure.

I want to talk to Paul and James and talk and talk some more.

I want to speak with the angels, put my cheek to a lion's paw,
and watch the films of the exodus and the flood
from the heavenly video store.
I want to see how creation occurred, and yet there's so much more;
and in it all, I'll encounter God; of that one thing I'm sure.

But will I have time for prayer in heaven? Surely that's the reason I'm there.
Yet, there's so much to do, I'm not sure I'll have time to spare.
But still, I should pray. There must be a time to stop and say
a few words to the Lord in prayer.

But I sense him saying that my whole life there
will be one big encounter with him.
Wherever I go, he'll have been there
before, and his perfume will fill every place,
and the people I see and talk to will reflect all the time his grace
and although I'll not see his face, God will still embrace me and trace
within my heart and mind the finger of love, the finger of grace.

I won't need to pray in heaven. Prayer won't bring me to God.
He'll be in everyone, everything, every sight, every song that I sing.
He'll be there in the acts and the deeds.
He'll be there in the sights that I see.
He'll be there in the plans that I have for the future,
the talks that I have about the past.
The places I'll go to, he's been to, and he'll be in the bits in

between.
Everywhere I go, God will say 'Hello'.
I'll encounter him without trying.
Without prayer, he'll still be there;
the consciousness of God will be like the air.

Maybe there'll be no prayer meetings in heaven
but prayer as it was meant to be;
responding to God in encounters he's planned
with me in mind, a mere speck in the sand.

For all eternity, he'll be whispering 'Hello'
in everyone around me and everywhere I go.

Questions for discussion

1. Does God enjoy it when we pray to him? (Deut 4:7; Job 33:26; Acts 10:4; 1 Pet 3:12)

2. Can we change God's mind when we pray? (Matt 26:39,42; 1 John 5:14)

3. What are some of the purposes of prayer? (Ps 32:6,7; Jer 42:3; Dan 6:11; 9:4,5; Acts 1:24; 6:6; 28:8; Phil 1:9–11; Col 4:3,4; James 5:16; 1 John 1:9)

4. What kinds of prayer does God appreciate? (1 Chron 5:20; Prov 15:8,29; James 5:16)

5. Where is God speaking today? (Ps 19:1–4)

Questions to think about

1. Should we pray to the Father, to Jesus, or to the Spirit, or doesn't it matter?

2. Why is prayer important for Christians?

3. Does it matter how long we pray or when we pray?

4. Is praying together more significant than praying on your own?

5. How should Christians listen for God in prayer?

13 Where do we go from here?

Things to remember:

- God is unimaginable, but he has invited you to explore him
- He wants you to know him more deeply than you ever thought possible
- Knowing God is potentially the most enjoyable quest in life
- We shall be exploring God for all eternity. Start now!
- Contemplating God will change you
- As you reflect on God, he will be reflected through you
- God has provided you with conversational partners in this exploration. Use all the resources they offer:
  The Holy Spirit
  The Bible
  Church leaders
  Friends
  Creation
  Your imagination and creative skills
  Life's experiences
  Art
  Poetry

Things to do:

Ask God to help you to explore him.

- Every day, thank him for a different aspect of his character
- Read a book about God
- Write a poem about God or his relationship with you
- Meditate on a Bible verse that describes God
- Slowly read aloud some Bible verses that explore aspects of God
- Enrol on a course exploring God
- Think about God for two or three minutes at a time
- Ask a friend: 'What is the most important aspect about God to you, and why?'
- Study one aspect of God that intrigues you
- Use a concordance to look at every verse in the Bible that records a particular aspect of God
- Try to discover the depth of meaning in God's love, holiness and power
- In conversation with some friends, complete the statement, 'God is ...'
- Express an aspect of God in a painting or drawing
- Compose a song about a characteristic of God
- Imagine a world without God
- Learn to listen for God in life
- Try to describe God as if you were speaking to these different people: a child, someone who has no concept of God, someone who has lost hope, and someone who is starting the journey
- Ask some older Christians: 'What are the three most important aspects of God to you?'
- Read some hymns that ponder the person of God
- Learn to wonder about God by asking questions like these:
  Could God be better?
  Where is God?
  How endless is his love?

How is God reflected in a leaf, a storm, the night, death?

When Jesus died, abandoned by all he'd known and loved,
his life had crashed to oblivion, it seemed, ignored by
heaven above.
The words on the lips of his followers as they gazed on his
cross on high
were words of sorrow that Good Friday; they whispered to
him, 'Goodbye.'

His mission at that moment had ended; a dirge seemed the
appropriate song
for all he'd lived and planned and dreamed; all of it had
gone.
But you and I know that not all was lost; his critics were
proved wrong
for when he died, Jesus Christ was simply passing on.

He moved; changed place, location; from Saviour to High
Priest.
His time on earth had finished; the star had moved from
the East
and followed him in all his life, in all his deeds had shone;
but now he's the Son in the heavens, for the Father has
moved him on.

He came to live, to love, to loose,
He came to fight and to win.
He came to feel for the pain of mankind,
to be spoiled with the stain of our sin.
And he came to show us the Father
for he was the Father's Son
and to say to us in his life and his death
that the Father was moving him on.

And in all you do, wherever you go,
when life's good and when it goes wrong;
whatever the valley, whatever the joy,
whatever the tune of your song,
the One who's in charge of this world and you
is the one who looked after his Son
and the pathway in life for all children of his
is always to be moving on.
With God, moving back is a feature
that does not fit into his plan.
He's much more concerned with the future,
with the lie and the range of the land that's ahead.
The past you've walked in – it's gone.
To the Father of Jesus you belong.

As you say goodbye to the present and past,
even to dreams that you thought would last,
and as people are saying goodbye, then they're gone
and you're left alone, very much on your own,
listen to the voice of the one who's been there
as he speaks with a heart that is filled with his care:
'Come with me; we're on our way.
Your future is born.
We're passing from this place;
I'm moving you on.'